Heidi Lanz

Ulrich Inderbinen

Translated by Richard and Regine Davy
– with thanks to Ian Trapp –

Rotten Verlag

Typesetting, printing, lithography: Mengis Druck und Verlag, Visp
Bound by: Eibert AG, Eschenbach SG
Front cover picture: Urs Möckli
Back cover picture: Silvano Armanini

ISBN 3-907816-50-1

"I am as old as the century"

This remark comes from the oldest active mountain guide in the world, Ulrich Inderbinen, who was born on 3 December 1900 and was still taking climbers up the Matterhorn at the age of 82. Until 1996 one could still encounter him in summer on
"four-thousanders" (peaks of over 4,000 metres), such as the Breithorn, Weissmies or
Allalinhorn.

He gave up his second profession, that of ski guide, only in 1995 but continued
climbing in summer. Every spring he would make a trial ascent of one of his favourite
mountains, the Breithorn, to test whether he was fit to undertake further expeditions.
Until 1996 he returned happy with confirmation that he could still go on.

In the summer of 1995 Ulrich climbed the Allalinhorn with two female compan-
ions. The ladies admit that when they reached the summit their guide was fresh and
cheerful while they were fairly tired and breathless. It is not surprising that the famous
guide has countless admirers of his extraordinary achievements. Foremost among
these are Heidi Lanz and Liliane De Meester, to whom we owe this biography.

For years the two ladies begged the old man to tell them something of his long life.
Ulrich Inderbinen's modesty is legendary, and he resisted for a long time – constantly
repeating that there was nothing worth special mention in his life. He had made no
spectacular first ascents, nor had he any other distinctive mountaineering achievements to his credit. But when he was 80 he was already recognised as a unique phe-
nomenon, and that period he regards as his best time.

It is thanks to Liliane De Meester, who has climbed with Ulrich since 1974, and her
friend Heidi Lanz that valuable notes and pictures have been preserved depicting the
life of Ulrich Inderbinen and the development of Zermatt to a world-renowned
mountain resort. I admire these two women who, with painstaking care, have collec-
ted old documents and photos from every imaginable archive in Switzerland and
abroad. The author, Heidi Lanz, was particularly well-equipped for this thorough
research because she studied journalism and German philology.

Since one of the aims of the Rotten Verlag is to foster and disseminate knowledge of
the customs and characteristics of the Valais it counts itself lucky to be able to publish
this biography of the oldest mountain guide in the world.

Ferdinand Mengis, Publisher

Ulrich Inderbinen with the bronze bust by Jean-Pierre Sandoz

I am often asked how, at my advanced age, I have been able to continue working as a mountain guide. Ever since I climbed the Matterhorn a few months before my ninetieth birthday I have been regularly asked for my "secret formula".

The answer may disappoint. I have never seen myself as a high-performing sportsman. I have never followed a special diet or done hard physical training. When the weather permits I walk every day for a few hours, preferably up the mountains. As for food, I am an uncomplicated person. I eat and drink everything in moderation.

My good health I attribute above all to my positive attitude to life, my enjoyment of nature, and my profession. As a child I learnt to be satisfied with little, to make no demands on life and always to work.

Thanks to my regular clients I have worked continuously as a mountain guide for 70 years. In July 1995 I made more than a dozen ascents of the Breithorn and the Allalin, both "four-thousanders". But since my seventy-fifth birthday I have had to give up my favourite tours to the Zinalrothorn and the Obergabelhorn. Difficult climbs, as well as ice and rock faces, I leave to younger people.

Except in the summer season my life runs a quiet course. My daily routine is regular. Stress and haste are unknown to me. I live as I climb mountains: at a pace that is slow and deliberate but also purposeful and regular. Among my colleagues I am known for not liking to stop before I reach my destination.

I still have plans for the future but I also like looking back on my life. I am therefore happy about this biography that describes my childhood and youth up to the Second World War.

For this exploration of my past I thank the author, Heidi Lanz, as well as Liliane De Meester, without whose support the book would not have been written.

Foreword

It was in the summer of 1993, after an expedition to the Breithorn, that we first told our distinguished guide that he should have written a book about his life. We pointed out that he was not only an exceptional mountain guide but also witness to a century in which his native village had developed into one of the most sought-after holiday resorts in Switzerland. Ulrich's reply was brief and typically self-mocking: "What, me, write a book? I'm happy that I can even read a book." For him that was the end of the matter.

At the beginning of 1995 we risked another attempt. January seemed the best time as Ulrich's activities were then curtailed by the weather. This time we had better luck. He was prepared to talk and we persuaded him to help us write his biography. "But there's not much about me that can't be told in a couple of sentences," he insisted.

Over the next five months we met him on two afternoons a week. Although by that time he was 94 years old, he answered innumerable questions with great patience and astonishing powers of recall, giving precise explanations of photos from the early years of the century and taking us to the hamlets above Zermatt where he spent his childhood.

From June onwards he was unable to give us any more time because he had to train for the international mountain guides' ski race in which he had participated every year since 1982. As usual he won – in his age group, in which he was the only competitor.

After that he had to prepare for the approaching summer season. From July to September he again led his long-time regular clients up his local mountains, climbing one of the snow-covered "four-thousanders" several times a week.

On 3 December 1995 the oldest inhabitant of Zermatt celebrated his ninety-fifth birthday. From all over the world he received the congratulations of friends, acquaintances and clients, several of whom took the opportunity to book a climb for the summer of 1996. Many strangers responded to one of the many newspaper articles about him by sending elaborate cards to their idol. Among the numerous gifts were practical things for his everyday needs, such as a rope and an ice-axe. He would certainly use them, as he made frequent use of the skis that his colleagues gave him for his ninetieth birthday.

After the excitement of his birthday had died down Ulrich again devoted himself to this book. He captioned the photos in his own handwriting and supplied us with more valuable information. For his assistance and the wonderful hours we spent together we thank him with all our hearts.

Heidi Lanz and Liliane De Meester

> *"This melancholy area needs only some dwellings that offer a few comforts to make it the top natural park in the world."*
>
> Prior Murith, 1810

Written records of the Inderbinen family of Zermatt go back to the middle of the seventeenth century. The names, dates of marriages and numbers of children are documented in Zermatt family records for seven generations before the birth of Ulrich Inderbinen. Moreover from these records, the dates of birth and death can be obtained back to and including the generation of his great-grandparents. But there are few other facts about his forebears. Like all Zermatters in those years they led the simple life of mountain farmers.

The native population of Zermatt was first described in the writings of visiting naturalists in the eighteenth century. One of the earliest reports comes from the *Journal de Paris* in the year 1777. An enthusiastic reader writes that in the Swiss settlement of Zermatt he has rediscovered the legendary "Golden Age". He portrays the "fortunate" inhabitants as "a truly liberated people without class divisions, without the torment of worldly ambition or luxuries to disturb them – a people who, shielded by their mountain fortress, live out their days in profound peace, concerned only with cultivating the land and tending their livestock".

Yet this idyllic picture could scarcely have corresponded to reality. In several other accounts Zermatt is described as one of the saddest villages in the valley, with unprofitable agriculture and deep poverty among the indigenous mountain farmers. In 1886 the *Neue Zürcher Zeitung* carried an article about a mountain guide from Zermatt who, "on the lovely Bürgenstock above Lake Lucerne, threw himself weeping onto the grass. His companion asked if he was in pain. 'No,' he explained, 'I am crying because the world is so beautiful here and so dismal at home'".[1]*

The declining population until the middle of the nineteenth century proves that the modest returns from agriculture were not sufficient to feed the inhabitants. Whereas the first official census in 1798 finds 600 "souls" in the isolated mountain village, by 1850 there were only 369. Poverty had forced many families to emigrate, causing several family lines to die out. Only after 1850, with the growth of the tourist industry

---

* The figures refer to the footnotes on p. 178 ff.

and new sources of income, did the population begin slowly but steadily to increase.

Zermatt in the nineteenth century

Ulrich Inderbinen's grandparents witnessed the beginnings of Alpine sport and the growth of tourism, yet when his maternal grandfather, Johann Josef Biner, was born in 1804 there were still no hotels in the village. In a holiday account from this period the botanist Murith writes that the only private accommodation to be found in Zermatt was at the house of one Josef Brenni. A few years later travellers could spend the night with the local priest where "something like a guest room was prepared" (*Journal de Zermatt,* 1901). The first guest house, with .three

12

beds, was opened in 1839. Ten or twelve visitors a year who journeyed to Zermatt on foot or by mule wrote their names in the visitors' book. The preconditions for developing tourism were finally provided in 1852 with the building of the first hotel.

Tourism still had no significance for Ulrich's grandparents. They lived like their forebears, largely self-sufficient from agriculture and animal husbandry. In the summer months, when botanists, mountaineers and health-seekers came to Zermatt, they were fully occupied working hard on the high, steep fields which extended in terraces to an altitude of over 2,000 metres.

Ulrich can provide little information about his grandparents. Both his grandfathers and one of his grandmothers were already dead when he was born, although they lived beyond the average life expectancy of that time. Johann Josef Biner died at 70, his wife Maria Luisa, known as Aloysia, at 78. His grandfather Moritz Inderbinen, born in 1817, was 72 when he died. No date is recorded for the death of his wife, Crescentia. The big gap between Ulrich's generation and that of his grandparents is a result of both grandfathers having surviving children only from their second marriages. At that time women had short life expectancy. Married women, especially, tended to die young, often during childbirth, leaving their husbands to start new families in their later years. In many native families a gap of 40 or more years is to be found between generations.

The first wife of Johann Josef Biner died childless after 27 years of marriage. At the age of 60 her widowed husband married 31-year-old Aloysia Aufdenblatten and they had five children. The third of these children was Ulrich's mother, Maria, born in 1869. Because of the large difference in the ages of his grandparents Ulrich knew only his grandmother Aloysia, who died when he was eleven.

Ulrich's grandfather Moritz also married twice. After he lost his first wife in the ninth year of their wedded life he married Crescentia Zumtaugwald in 1853. The couple had six children, all of whom lived for more than 70 years; the youngest daughter died at 93. Ulrich's father, Hieronymus, who was born the fifth child in 1866, lived to be 90.

A glance over the Zermatt family statistics reveals not only the striking frequency of deaths among young women at that time but also extremely high infant mortality. The causes are given in old parish records princi-

Die Bahnhofstrasse von Zermatt

ca. 1890

Bahnhofstrasse (main street), Zermatt

pally as frailty at birth or in childhood, influenza and pneumonia. Families in which several children died were not exceptional; one couple at the beginning of the nineteenth century lost 13 out of 15 children.

430	1799	Johannes Zurniwen, born no. 427.
		Maria Salzgeber, born no. 324.
	1802	Johannes, twice married no. 431 and 432.
	1808	Anna Maria, married Peter Inderbinen, no. 163.
		Another 13 children, of whom 12 boys, who preferred to go straight to Heaven rather than remain longer in this wicked world.

Extract
from family statistics
by J. Ruden

Because of the isolation of the village medical help often arrived too late. The nearest doctor was 22 miles away in Visp. The road through the valley was only in places wide enough for a carriage, so the sick had to be put on a stretcher for many miles or transported by mule. Those too ill to be moved were in a hopeless predicament. With the opening of the Visp–Zermatt railway in 1891 the sick could be transported easily as far as Visp, but only in summer. Later they could also be taken on by connecting trains to the new hospital which opened in Brig in 1908.

A distinct improvement came in 1909, when a doctor set up practice in Zermatt, but for ailments requiring an operation the situation remained precarious for a long time. Until the train started winter services in 1929 it closed from November to May. In those months Zermatt was often completely cut off from the outside world by heavy snowfalls and avalanches. Then an illness such as appendicitis was effectively a death sentence. Many small children died in winter from their first influenza.

In the *Journal de Zermatt* of June 1904 a villager complains about the hardship that "winter's evil power inflicts on us poor wretches, cut off from the world, when the steam locomotive says farewell with its bone-piercing whistle at midnight on 1 November." There follows a description of the cold, snowy winter: "The telegraph wires were down, the post was stopped by avalanches and rock slides; thus at least we were not bothered by the bailiff. But what happens when someone gets ill? He has to find his way to the next world without medical help".[2]

Ulrich's father also had a sad experience as a result of these conditions. In 1889, at the age of 23, he married Regina Welschen, born in 1860. Over the next five years Regina had four children, none of whom was to reach adulthood. The first child, a son, died of frailty in March 1890, shortly after birth. The second, a girl, Balbina, survived only to the age of ten. The third and fourth lived just a few days. In 1895, a year after her last child was buried, Regina Inderbinen died of jaundice, leaving her husband with four-year-old Balbina.

"We were three boys and each had six sisters."

For two years Hieronymus lived alone with the little girl before he married 28-year-old Maria Biner. In 1898 the couple had a son, Albinus, and a year later a daughter, Maria.

Early in 1899 Hieronymus began to build a house on the left bank of the village river, the Vispa, together with his brother Moritz and his

Zermatt in 1899. In the centre foreground is the site where my parents built the "Villa Vispa".

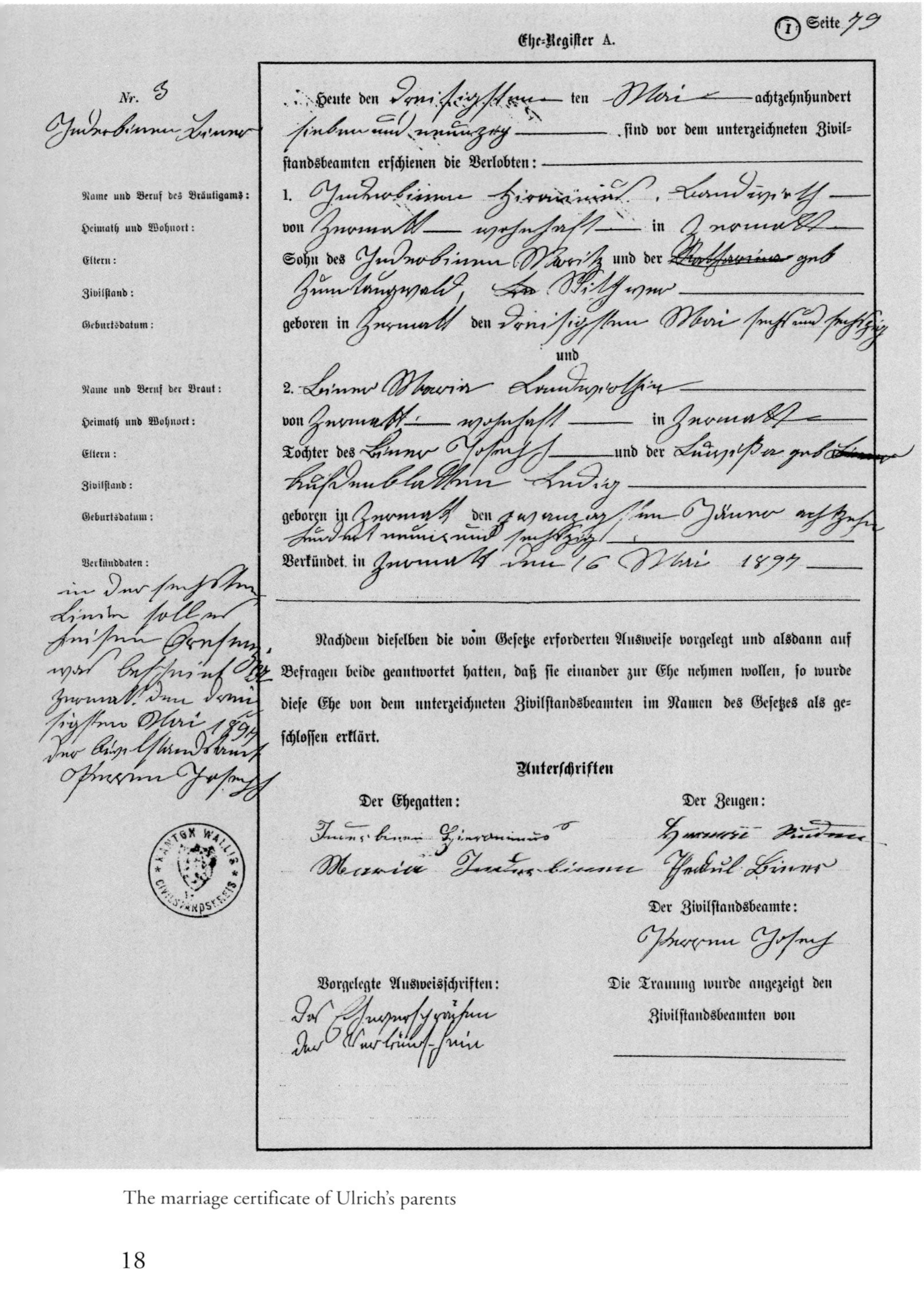

Ehe-Register A. Seite 79

Nr. 3

Heute den … ten … achtzehnhundert … sind vor dem unterzeichneten Zivilstandsbeamten erschienen die Verlobten:

Name und Beruf des Bräutigams: 1. …

Heimath und Wohnort: von … wohnhaft in …

Eltern: Sohn des … und der …

Zivilstand: …

Geburtsdatum: geboren in … den …

und

Name und Beruf der Braut: 2. …

Heimath und Wohnort: von … wohnhaft in …

Eltern: Tochter des … und der …

Zivilstand: …

Geburtsdatum: geboren in … den …

Verkünddaten: Verkündet in … den 16 Mai 1897

Nachdem dieselben die vom Gesetze erforderten Ausweise vorgelegt und alsdann auf Befragen beide geantwortet hatten, daß sie einander zur Ehe nehmen wollen, so wurde diese Ehe von dem unterzeichneten Zivilstandsbeamten im Namen des Gesetzes als geschlossen erklärt.

Unterschriften

Der Ehegatten: …

Der Zeugen: …

Der Zivilstandsbeamte: …

Vorgelegte Ausweisschriften: …

Die Trauung wurde angezeigt den Zivilstandsbeamten von …

KANTON WALLIS CIVILSTANDSKREIS

The marriage certificate of Ulrich's parents

brother-in-law Josef Biner. In less than two years they finished the "Villa Vispa". The house was typical of the Valais region, with one side of wood and the others of stone. The staircase was located outside the building to save a few square metres of space. In those days it was usual for several families to build a house together as no one had the money to construct their own house. Each family then occupied one floor.

Ulrich Inderbinen's birth certificate

On 3 December 1900 at ten o'clock in the morning Ulrich came into the world. Like his brother and sister he was born at home with the assistance of a midwife, Maria Lauber. Whether this was in the new house or in his parents' apartment in the house "am Schtizzje" is not known. The same afternoon the infant was baptised by pastor Benedikt Zurbrig-

The old church in which I was christened. It was demolished in 1913 and replaced by a new church.

gen at the font in the old village church. He was the first child in Zermatt to be given the name Ulrich. Why his parents chose this name, which was unusual at the time, Ulrich does not know. Present at the baptism, besides Hieronymus Inderbinen, were the godparents Theodul Biner, a good friend of his father, and Katharina Kronig, a distant relation. Maria Inderbinen could not attend the ceremony so soon after giving birth. Like all mothers she had to be churched by the priest before she was allowed to enter church again.

Ulrich was born during an exceptionally cold winter. For several days in February the temperature sank to –27 degrees Centigrade. More than 11 miles of the Vispa river were frozen over. The bitter cold caused little Balbina, Ulrich's half-sister from his father's first marriage, to become very ill. She died in February 1901 at the age of ten. With her passing Hieronymus lost the fifth and last member of his first family.

In the following years the Inderbinen family expanded but two more children died. In 1902 a fourth child, Ulrich's sister Martha, was born, and two years later his brother Otto, who died from influenza a month after birth. In 1905 Franziska was born, and in 1906 Berta followed, but she also survived only a few weeks. In 1908 came another girl, christened Berta after her deceased sister. In 1909 Maria Inderbinen gave birth to

Family records showing the birth dates of Hieronymus Inderbinen's children, the marriage of Albinus and the childless marriage of Franz Inderbinen (the brother of Ulrich's grandfather Moritz) in 1845. The note reads: "This Franz was hired on 25 September 1848 by a man from Gressoney to carry a pack over the Theodul Glacier. On this trip he disappeared. How and where only God knows."

578	1897	Hieronymus Jnderbinen, geb. No 161, II. Ehe. Maria Biner, geb. No 538.
	1898	Albinus, geb. No 578A.
	1899	Maria, geh. Biner Theodor, No 544.
	1900	Ulrich.
	1902	Martha, geh. Gehrig Arnold, v. Amriswil, Aarg.
	1905	Franziska.
	1908	Berta.
	1909	Monika.
	1911	Medard.
	1914	Veronika.
578A	1926	Albinus Jnderbinen, geb. No 578. Melania Lauber, geb. No 1014.
162	1845	Franz Jnderbinen, geb. No 157. Katharina Furrer, geb. No 130. } Kinderlos (1)

(1) Diefer Franz wurde 1848 den 25, Sept. von einem Manne aus Greßoney gedungen einen Pack über den Theodulgletscher zu tragen, auf welcher Reise er verschwand. Wie und wo ist Gott bekannt.

5

Monika, in 1911 Medard was born and finally, in 1914, the last child, Veronika. With her arrival the Inderbinen family had grown to eleven members. To emphasise the predominance of girls, Ulrich, even in old age, still replies to enquiries about his brothers and sisters with the words: "We were three boys and each of us had six sisters".

"The English predominated in Zermatt, particularly the aristocrats."
F. O. Wolf, 1886

Ulrich and his brothers and sisters were born into a growing holiday resort. At the turn of the century the village had 741 inhabitants, so the population had doubled within 50 years. Since the tragic first ascent of the Matterhorn in July 1865, when four people lost their lives, Zermatt had become known throughout the world and developed quickly into a popular summer health resort. The number of visitors increased markedly with the opening of the railway between Visp and Zermatt in 1891, and again after 1898 with the inauguration of the first electric mountain train in the world, the Gornergrat Railway, which reached an altitude of more than 3,000 metres. Even in its first year of operation the Visp–Zermatt railway carried 33,000 passengers. By the year of Ulrich's birth the annual number had already reached 51,000.

In that period there were about 20 hotels and guest houses in Zermatt and they were always overcrowded in summer. Overnight accommodation in a simple hotel cost 4–5 francs, while a night in the luxurious Hotel Zermatt came to 8 francs. Electric lighting cost an additional 1–2 francs a week.

In the year of Ulrich's birth a lot of building was in progress. Several hotels were reconstructed or enlarged. The only stone dwelling house in Zermatt at that time, known as the White House, was pulled down and later replaced by the Villa Margherita in which the post-office was housed. In the summer of 1900 Zermatt was given its first twelve telephone connections. In the same year the local authority built a new village hall, began constructing a sewage system and replaced the cobbles in

ZERMATT

VALAIS
(SUISSE)
Altitude 1620 metres.

Station Alpestre et Climatérique ⟨⟩ d'une réputation universelle.

Centre unique d'excursions et ascensions dans les Alpes

FLORE RARE ET TRÈS VARIÉE — GÉOLOGIE INTÉRESSANTE

**Station recommandée par la plupart des médecins
pour son air pur, salubre
et vivifiant et la rareté des pluies.**

offre les tableaux les plus grandioses du monde des glaciers

Excursions superbes à pied et à cheval. Chemin de fer des plus pittoresques de Viège à Zermatt. — Médecin. Pharmacie. — Jeux, Orchestre, et en général toutes les ressources et installations qu'offrent les stations de 1er ordre, tant au point de vue des distractions que de l'hygiène. — Culte catholique. Eglise anglaise. Service protestant en français et en allemand.

Hôtels à Zermatt

Grand Hôtel Mont-Cervin	
Grand Hôtel de Zermatt	
Hôtel Mont-Rose	
Hôtel Ryffelalp, sur le Ryffel (2227ᵐ)	Tenus par
Hôtel Ryffelberg (2569ᵐ)	
Horel Schwarzsee (2589ᵐ)	la famille Seiler
Buffet de la Gare	
Restaurant Belvédère, au sommet du Gornergrat (3137ᵐ)	
Hôtel Terminus	M. Dol-Lauber.
Hôtel Victoria	M. De Preux.
Hôtel Bellevue	M. Gsponer.
Hôtel Schweizerhof	
Hôtel de la Poste	MM. Mathier & Gattlen.
Hôtel d'Angleterre	M. de Preux.

Extract from *Journal de Zermatt,* 1900

A side street in Zermatt at the turn of the century. The old cemetery was moved before
the new church was built.

the Bahnhofstrasse with asphalt. In the *Journal de Zermatt* of September
1900 the removal of the cobbles was welcomed because they had been "a
constant source of suffering for the sore feet of the tourists". With the exception of the Bahnhofstrasse none of the roads in Zermatt was as-
phalted; the small side-alleys were only partly reinforced with cobble

stones. Because of their bad condition, Edward Whymper advised readers of his travel guide to Zermatt not to venture off the main street.

At the turn of the century around 170 mountain guides worked from Zermatt. "From early morning to late in the evening they sat or stood in front of the hotels and tried to sell their services to the tourists as guides, porters, chair bearers, coach drivers or escorts" (*Journal de Zermatt*, 1902). A guide earned around 100 francs for an ascent of the Matterhorn, a porter around 70 francs. The ten fatal accidents that had occurred on the Matterhorn up to the year 1900 justified the good remuneration. The rates for simple excursions were considerably lower. The eight-hour ascent of the Breithorn paid only 25 francs. The wages of chair bearers and mule drivers were also modest, but humans were slightly cheaper than mules. A tourist could be carried by two chair bearers to the Schwarzsee and back for only 8 francs, whereas anyone wishing to cover the same route on a mule had to pay 10 francs.

Chair bearers on their way up to Gornergrat

Die Dorfstrasse vor dem Hotel Monte Rosa

26

1905

The village street in front of the Monte Rosa hotel

Ulrich's father had worked a few times as a chair bearer before he was married. Later he told his children about this exhausting work. The three-hour climb to the Schwarzsee had to be accomplished by only two bearers. The climb from Zermatt to Gornergrat, which was almost double the distance, required four bearers who could relieve each other. Before the construction of the Gornergrat railway there were 60–70 mules in action, carrying up to 18,000 people a year to the Gornergrat.[3]

There are several vivid accounts of Zermatt at this time. In his book *The Matterhorn,* published in 1905, the noted alpinist Guido Rey writes: "In Zermatt the old and the new are not in harmony. The grand hotels dwarf the little cottages of the old days, and the bright whitewash of the new buildings makes the fine, dark wood of the old rain-washed, sun-baked dwellings seem shabby. The large hotel carriages which pick up visitors at the station take up half the road and confuse the herds of placid cattle that pass through the village... A hundred small stalls stand before the houses along the only street in the village selling every type of alpine goods."

The mountaineer Theodor Wundt lamented the end of the good old times "when mountaineering was still not marred by so many by-products of over-civilisation... From year to year the flood of visitors increased. All kinds of fashionable clothes appeared, concerts and balls were introduced. The good old days were gone forever".

Others saw the development of Zermatt with less critical eyes, calling it the "pearl of the Alps", the "queen of alpine resorts", "paradise on earth", a "radiant Thebaid",[4] the "mountaineers' Mecca", asserting that its rustic and natural character had not been destroyed by a few big hotels. All accounts describe the international mix of people in Zermatt and the daily cosmopolitan throng on the Gornergrat. According to Wundt the village became "a fashionable international health resort with visitors who were elegant, refined, reserved and often delicate". Many guide books emphasize the healthy climate of Zermatt and promise an immediate cure – or at least definite improvement – for those with nervous conditions, hysteria and insomnia. "Someone suffering genuine migraine can expect release even on the day of arrival in the high mountains. Debilitating cases of hysteria, melancholy and epilepsy have also shown marked improvement." *(Journal de Zermatt, 1907).*

In the year 1900 about 90% of visitors came from abroad. A third were English, 21% German, 13% French, 11% American and Canadians. The rest were Italians, Austrians and tourists from Belgium, the Netherlands and Luxembourg.[5] With the opening of the Simplon tunnel in June 1906 the number of Italian visitors rose sharply. A new era began: "The Italians have come with their families, children and nannies or in groups with parents, friends and acquaintances. Very jolly, a bit noisy, elegantly dressed, they have totally changed the appearance of the village."[6] Very slowly the traditional life of the villagers began to change as more and more farmers gave up their work for jobs in the tourist industry. An article in the *Journal de Zermatt* in 1901 explained: "Agriculture is coming to be regarded more as a sideline. Everyone is turning to the tourist industry; that this is profitable is shown primarily by the many magnificent new private houses with their bright, spacious accommodation and pleasant interiors. In the last ten years alone, 66 such new dwellings have been built. Assuming an average value of 5,000 francs each, this represents a total value of 330,000 francs.... yet this is only a small proportion of the newly created wealth."

"We were the last nomads"

Maria and Hieronymus Inderbinen did not succumb to the great temptation to exchange farming for lucrative work in tourism. They adhered to their simple lifestyle and remained self-sufficient, poor but independent. Their own agricultural produce was just sufficient to feed the family and livestock, and to provide reserves for the long winter. There was no surplus to sell. Only by marketing a sheep or a calf could some money be earned, primarily to have shoes made. Money was also needed to buy the food they could not produce themselves. Ulrich's mother bought rice, polenta, maccaroni, sugar, salt, tea and coffee in one of the small shops in the village.

The family's diet was simple and healthy. Bread was baked with their own rye flour; potatoes and vegetables were home-grown. The hens provided eggs for the family, and the cows gave milk from which mother

Mr et Mme Buckley et famille 5 pers. England
Her. Franz Schalk k. k. Holfkapell- meister Wien
Frau L. Schalk kind u. Bedienung
Baron et baronne de la Boulaye France
Her. und Frau Schnorf-Zuppinger Zürich
Fräuleins Schnorf
M. et Mme Delachaux Neuchâtel
M. Rieder „
Mrs Jaylor London
Dr jur. Barkenhausen und Frau Breemen
M. Armand La Haye
Mme Armand „
Her. Bofvat, Dr Schwarz und Frau Baden-Baden
M. le Comte de Keranflech „
Mme la Ctesse de Keranfl„ch „
M. Dr Beuckiser Karlsruhe
M. Huaptmann von Dommes Berlin
Mr et Mrs S. Young London
Mme Keuer Kiel
Mlle Koudmann New-York
M Deugler Wien
M Sauvage Paris
M Clément Sauvage „
Mrs Bume Baltimore
Mr H. Eccleston „
Mr et Mrs Courvor Boston
M. André Lyon et famille France
Dr Seidler et familie 5 pers Berlin
M. W. Hirsemann Leipzig
Miss Shepherd Angleterre
Miss Witteaus „
Mr et Mrs Ridewood „
M. Gaston Tuvée Paris
M Bernatz Wien
Mme Rieder „
M. Ryde and party 5 pers. England
Mr Suyden San Francisco
Dr méd. Schneer et Frl. Neapel
M. Général von Dommes Hanover

Mr Parmentier Bosto
Mr Dana „
Mme Howault Lyc
Mr et Mrs Monteagel Manchest
Sig. Dr F. Soldi Genr
Mme Soldi „
Mme et Mlle Maria Guida „
Mlle P. Agosti „
Mlle Anah Febvre Lyc
Marquis et Mquise de Monte Silva Napl
M. Josef von Sieberts Wie
Miss Bonsor Lond
M. Picard Par
M. Allé Hal
Frl. von Breidenbug Darmsta
Famille Sacchi 3 pers. Mila
Famille Uboldi 5 pers. „
M. Eduard Berndt Wi
Mr Macdonald Lond
Mr John Hunter „
M. Malet Fran
M. Kuentzi Pa
Mr et Mrs M. Cacl Edinbur
M. Ernst Schuhmacher Hannov
M. Adolph Schugmayer „
M. Barrot Ly
Mlles Ziffet Wi
M. et Mme Grevosd St-Mich
Mme Léonville „
Dr et Mrs Gilfillau New-Yo
M. Hard, premier président Pa
Dr Pf. Schaeffer Coble
M. Braumühl Rheinla
M. Blot et famille Pa
M. et Mrs Platner U S
Sig. Carlo Fransco Tori
M. et Mme Marthouret et fam. 6 pe Ly
Mme David Winter Pa
M. Crémieux et famille Pa
M. et Mme Horaud Ly
Prof. Dr et Mme Stoppaur Zuri
Mme Verburgt La Ha
M. le Chanoine le Faud Nam

au u. Frl. Weill	Francfort	M. et Mme Léopold Krämer	„
. Rudolph	„	M. et Mme Trommitz	Rheinland
. Young	London	Dr Heineeke	Leipzig
. et Mme Lamy	Paris	Dr P. Glockeuer	„
. et Mme Ibach	Barmen	M. l'abbé Favre	St-Etienne
. Galibert	France	M. l'abbé Nauais	„
. Fernet	„	Dr Barkhausen	Bremen
H. Schaefer	Francfort	Frl. Kutsche	Neisse
. Dufouleur	Nuits	Frl. Zedler	„
. le Comte et Comtesse de la Selle		Frl. Haward	„
et famille	Paris	M. Armand	La Haye
M. et Mmes Stoppani	Turin	M. Georg Graethnysen	Freiburg
. Gunther u. Sohn	Francfort	M. Heim	„
. Pfarrer Dettmenig	„	M. le Dr et Mme Audigé	Paris
. et Mme Schulet	Alexandrie	M. et Mme Hofrat Sifmuwg	Baden
r et Mrs Lones	Brooklyn	Mme Clara Leithold	Berlin
r et Mrs Perterson	Chicago	Mme Dora Muller	„
und Frau Schuhmacher	Berlin	M. le Comte et Ctesse de Kerauffech	
me Paul Voinier	Nancy		France
ne Jules Sajor	„	M. R. Littchen	Pettersburg
Cambrillard et fils	Lyon	M. et Mme L. Gouy	Genève
. Falkmann	Cöln		
r Moses	„		
Albersheim	„		
Kaufmann	Hamburg		
au Neergaard	Copenhague		
rs et Misses Henry Sitchfield			
	New-York		
et Frau Vegelsaug	Francfort		
et Mme de Borredou	Paris		
Bernard de Borredou	„		
les de Borredou	„		
André de la Porte	La Haye		
ne Kersten			
ne Reraud	Harlem		
Kommerzienrat Lüst	Berlin		
Prof. Karewsky	„		
mte Guido Boelli	Turin		
. G. L. Pomba	„		
. Vittorio Cajana	„		
et Mme Gustav Kug	Wien		
Joseph Stichet	„		
Otto Kala	Baden-Baden		
Ventzel	Berlin		
Sauter	Zurich		

also made butter and cheese. Sausage and meat came from the slaughter of their own animals. The meat was heavily salted and hung in a store-room to dry. As a rule, animals were slaughtered only in the autumn, so dried meat was cooked and eaten throughout the year.

Fruit was only occasionally on the menu because no fruit trees grow at Zermatt's high altitude. On special occasions mother bought a few apples which were shared out fairly among the children. In summer the children hunted for wild fruits such as wild strawberries, raspberries and bilberries. In autumn, as a welcome change, they ate the small oily nuts from pine cones.

Only very seldom did Ulrich and his brothers and sisters get sweets. Their mother kept sugar out of their reach. It was purchased in a single hard, brown lump from which pieces had to be hacked off with a knife. The only substitute offered by nature was wild honey, which the children sometimes found in a bee's nest and consumed with great delight. Meals were taken together at set times. For breakfast at 6.30 a.m. there was milk and bread with a piece of cheese, or a gruel of butter, rye flour and water. In the middle of the day, at around 11.30 a.m., potatoes, vegetables and sometimes a little meat were eaten. In the evening the family assembled at six o'clock. The meal consisted of bread, a bit of sausage or again warm gruel. On Sundays and holidays the midday meal was more generous. Mother always prepared a cut of meat, and sometimes a pancake.

When the harvest was poor, soup replaced the main meal on many days. Worst was a bad rye harvest, which meant that flour, and consequently bread, were in short supply. Ulrich never had to go hungry but there was always little to eat. He found Lent particularly hard because meat was forbidden for 40 days. As a reward he and his siblings received a slice of sausage for breakfast on Easter Sundays.

Milk was not only an important part of the daily diet but also a cure-all for illnesses great and small. Once the children quarrelled over a 20 centime coin and one of them angrily swallowed it. The stomach pains were eased with a large glass of warm milk. For external injuries Maria Inderbinen fell back on traditional natural remedies. Open wounds got a plaster of stinging nettles; for bruises and sprains a resin-soaked cloth was applied. Ulrich's mother spread resin from the larch or Arolla pine onto a clean linen cloth. Then she melted the sticky mass with an iron into which she had thrust stones warmed in the oven. The cloth with lukewarm melted resin was finally wound around the injury as a bandage. This procedure proved particularly useful for animals. When a sheep had a broken leg, Hieronymus taped up the injured area with a resin-soaked cloth which hardened into a sort of plaster cast as the resin cooled.

Medicines were unknown in the Inderbinen family. Children's diseases, 'flu and toothache had to be endured; Ulrich's parents had little time to comfort their offspring. For all that, Ulrich enjoys looking back on his childhood, which he regards as the happiest time of his life. His was the last of Zermatt's "nomad" families. Although many of the villagers had a summer residence in one of the small hamlets above Zermatt, only Ulrich's family moved five times a year. Following the rhythm of the changing seasons they went to wherever there was work to be done in the fields.

At the end of April Maria and Hieronymus moved with their nine children, four cows and several hens from Zermatt to the small settlement of Blatten, half an hour's walk above the village. In June they moved on to Zmutt at an altitude of 1,940 metres, where they stayed for a few weeks to cultivate the fields. Then it was time for a third move to gather the harvest in Blatten and the surrounding area. In September the rye from the higher fields had to be brought in, so the "caravan" was on the move for the fourth time, making Zmutt again the family residence until shortly before Christmas. Only from the middle of December to April did they live in the Haus Vispa in Zermatt. The many moves earned them the nickname "Piöüktu", which can be translated as "the people in a hurry".

"Mountain folk! No other people are more lovingly attached to their home ground, nor cling more firmly to the faith of their fathers." Emil Yung, 1896

With the exception of a break on Sundays Ulrich saw his parents, especially his mother, do nothing but work. His mother got up at 4 a.m. to fetch water from the spring, tend the livestock and clear out the cowshed. She milked the cows, carried the heavy milk cans home, prepared meals for the large family, washed the laundry in the water trough, ironed, mended clothes, cleaned, helped in the fields and spun the sheep's wool on a spinning-wheel. In any "free" moment she knitted socks and stockings, gloves and pullovers for the children. Only on Sundays and holidays could she relax a little. Then even the knitting needles

My mother in front of our cellar in Blatten

had to rest. But essential work was allowed, such as tending the livestock and preparing meals. In spite of this hard life Maria never complained about her lot, which she shared with the other local women. She never left Zermatt, the place of her birth.

34

My mother in front of our house in Zmutt. My father is looking out of the window.

Ulrich's father also led a life of dutiful hard work, dominated by the worry of supporting a family with nine children. Every evening he planned the work for the next day, often causing his wife to remark "But first we sleep". Hieronymus never took a holiday; the only break from routine was his annual visit to the cattle markets in Stalden and Visp, where animals were bought, exchanged or sold.

Ulrich's father was a respected man in the village. After being sacristan for a long time he served eight years as treasurer on the local council. In his youth he had tended his father's sheep in winter. A "pioneering deed" of his was mentioned in several books: "In the 1880s an inhabitant of Zermatt came close to inventing skis. One morning the village awoke to two metres of new snow. Farmers with cattle in the high hamlets could not get through to feed them. Two days passed. By the third day it became impossible to leave the cattle alone any longer! The alpine herdsmen of Zum See reached their goal only in the late evening, even though eight men had taken turns to make a track through the snow. Hieronymus Inderbinen, however, who had a herd in Zmutt but was on his own, reached his cattle in half a day because he had the idea of tying boards to the soles of his shoes."[7]

The description which Theodor Wundt gave of the villagers in 1930 would also have applied to Ulrich's parents: "The Zermatter is a child of the raw, remote mountains of the Valais, an uncommonly strong, industrious and tough person, hard on himself, patriarchal and loyal to old customs. The power of Nature, to whose terrors and dangers he is exposed throughout the winter, has made him more deeply aware than other people of human impotence; it has overshadowed his character with an earnest and almost fatalistic devotion to God. Quiet and withdrawn, he goes his own way, never at any price missing Mass on Sundays and never passing a holy picture without saying a Hail Mary. Thus he stands in close relation to God, whom he confidently expects to hear his prayers. When, for example, a storm threatens or heavy snow falls in summer, the villagers are summoned by the bells of the village church and the smaller bells of the seven chapels that lie scattered around the valley and mountainsides. For an hour the villagers wail and lament. Then there is a pause. They pray some more and go outside to see if God has heard them. If he has not they ring the bells for another hour and pray

Mein Vater in seiner Sonntagskleidung
mit Nagelschuhen

My father in his Sunday best with nailed shoes

before looking out again. In this way the Zermatters converse with God. If He does not relent they go on ringing the bells for half a day, a whole day, several days; the heavens will tire before they do... Another conspicuous characteristic is an insurmountable aversion to everything unfamiliar, which they will oppose stubbornly with almost childish defiance."[8]

Ulrich and his siblings belonged to the last generation that addressed their parents formally. Any other way of talking would have been regarded as disrespectful. Maria and Hieronymus were devout Christians, and they raised their children as strict Catholics. Every evening they said prayers together. In winter they prayed the rosary for half an hour, in summer five Our Fathers and five Hail Marys. These so-called "Five Wounds", for the five wounds of Christ, took only ten minutes. Father recited the first half of the two prayers aloud and mother said the second half with the children.

The text of the rosary varied according to the days of the week. On Mondays and Thursdays they recited the "Five Joyful Mysteries of the Rosary", on Tuesdays and Fridays, the "Five Sorrowful Mysteries", and on Wednesdays and at weekends the "Five Glorious Mysteries". In addition, a short grace was said before and after meals.

Before mother cut a loaf she blessed it and made an incision in the form of a cross on the underside. No members of the family left the house without first crossing themselves with holy water.

On Sundays the parents went with their children to one of four morning masses. There was no breakfast on this day because they had to fast before receiving communion. "One must have an empty stomach when receiving Holy Communion, so one must eat nothing whatever after midnight before." This rule from the catechism was observed by everyone. The warning that "one should be respectably attired" was also heeded. The grown-ups and the children put on their Sunday best to go to church. Only their shoes could not be changed because everyone had only one pair.

In church there was a strictly observed seating arrangement. Ulrich's mother and his sisters sat with the other women to the left of the aisle, while he himself took his seat on the right with his father and brothers.

In the course of a year various religious festivals were celebrated, some of which were combined with a procession. The Inderbinen family regularly took part. The two biggest religious occasions were Corpus Christi on the second Thursday after Whitsun and the Chapel Festival on the fifth of August. The children liked the Corpus Christi procession best. It was led by soldiers and a band, followed by schoolboys carrying the flags of 22 cantons and girls dressed in white. The streets were decked with flowers, flags and garlands, and in front of the hotels stood altars at which the procession stopped to pray. Following the religious ceremony there was free wine at the community hall for the men of the village.

The Chapel Festival took place in the chapel of "Our Lady of the Snow" (Maria zum Schnee) at Schwarzsee, a lake high up the mountain near the foot of the Matterhorn. Every year the pilgrimage was made not only by the locals but also by the faithful from neighbouring villages. Additional processions were held when the harvest was threatened. If the summer was rainy, a procession went to the chapel in the hamlet of Findeln to "fetch the sun". When the summer was too dry it went up to the chapel of "Our Lady of the Snow" to pray for rain. Ulrich remembers that many of the faithful were so convinced of the effectiveness of such a pilgrimage that they took umbrellas with them.

Except on religious occasions Ulrich and his brothers and sisters did not come down to the village in summer. Their nomadic life left them relatively untouched by tourism. When they were living in Zermatt in winter there were virtually no tourists, and in summer, when the visitors came to Zermatt, the family was on the move. The summer concerts in the gardens of the big hotels, the elegant evening wear of the guests, the shop displays and the sumptuous meals in the hotels were all far removed from the everyday life of the Inderbinen family.

When, on 19 September 1903, the renowned Captain Spelterini made a spectacular flight by balloon from Zermatt to Bignasco in the Tessin, Hieronymus and Maria Inderbinen were working in the fields. Farming was for them more important than the "European spectacle", which attracted world-wide attention and brought many journalists and spectators to Zermatt.

The start of Captain Spelterini's balloon flight from Zermatt to Bignasco

"The abandoned hamlet was melancholy but in the midday heat the chirp of the surrounding crickets gave an impression of life." François Gos, 1925

The hamlet Blatten was Ulrich's favourite place. There the children did not have to share their kingdom with anyone because theirs was the only family in residence. The remaining houses and apartments stood empty; the owners came to cultivate the fields but returned to Zermatt in the evening.[9]

The house in which Ulrich spent the happiest time of his childhood had three dwellings belonging to different owners. Hieronymus Inderbinen's apartment on the first floor consisted of a kitchen and a parlour. As the number of children increased the two small rooms could no longer provide everyone with sleeping space, so Ulrich and his older brother Albinus slept in a nearby unoccupied house whose owners were good friends of the family. The cellar in this neighbouring house belonged to Ulrich's parents, while the cellar in their own house belonged to another family.

This arrangement was typical of the complicated property relations in Zermatt. To save money all buildings were normally constructed with several other families, but as the buildings were inherited by subsequent generations property became increasingly fragmented. For instance, a family might own a third of one house, a quarter of the cowshed beside the house, and one eighth of a storehouse in another place. In Blatten, the property of Ulrich's father also included a hen-house, a cowshed and

Blatten. In the centre of the picture is our house. On the rock on the left we children learnt to climb.

Our house in Blatten. In the annexe on the right were two empty dwellings.

42

waren zwei Wohnungen die leerstanden

The neighbour's house in which I and my brother Albinus slept.

Bruder Albinus schließen

half a barn, while the garden and fields directly in front of his house were divided among various other owners.

The different types of farm building that were used at that time still survive in Zermatt and surrounding hamlets. The barns or granaries *(Stadel)* are used to store grain. They have only one door and usually rest on six wooden posts with flat stones on top to prevent mice getting in. The storehouses *(Speicher)* are similar but usually have two storeys and more doors, and contain storage rooms in which food is stockpiled. Cowsheds *(Ställe,* also known as "Gädi"), have two storeys and usually three doors.

Die Kornfelder in Blatten

The cornfields in Blatten

With my sister on the bench in front of the tea-house

The lowest door lets in cattle or sheep, the upper one is used to throw in hay, and the middle one allows fodder to be taken out in winter.[10]

The small chapel behind the Inderbinens' house in Blatten dated from 1640. Every year on Ascension Day, the fortieth day after Easter, a Mass was said there, combined with a procession known as the "long procession". Almost every day Hieronymus, Maria and the children went to the chapel to pray for a few minutes.

At the side of the house stood a small restaurant. Ulrich and his brothers and sisters sometimes sat on a wooden fence and watched the well-dressed tourists drinking tea or coffee. It never occurred to them that they and their parents might also be entitled to holidays, relaxation and

Vorplatz der Kapelle in Blatten.
Das Mädchen im Vordergrund bin
ich im Jahre 1902.
Damals trugen auch die Jungen
in den ersten Lebensjahren Mädchenkleider.
Neben mir mein Bruder Albinus
und meine Schwester Maria

Forecourt of the chapel in Blatten. The "girl" in the foreground is me in 1902. In those days boys wore girls' clothes in their early years. Sitting near me are my brother Albinus and my sister Maria.

fine clothes. The *Journal de Zermatt* of August 1906 described the fashionable travellers who "carry in their rucksacks all sorts of useless junk like kettles, egg cups, clothes-brushes and so forth. A splendid example of this type was observed recently making the ascent with stiffly starched shirt front, stiff collar and patent-leather shoes".

A very special visitor who regularly spent the summer in Zermatt was the painter Albert Gos. Many of his landscape sketches were done in Blatten, where he sat with his easel in the forecourt of the small chapel. The children liked to watch him paint and sometimes posed for him. He arrived every year in May or June. Ulrich and his siblings waited eagerly for the day because the painter always brought them a sack full of presents. Each child in turn was allowed to reach inside the jute sack and take out one of the items. There were small toys such as marbles or carved figures and sometimes sweets, a luxury which Ulrich's parents could not afford. Often the artist brought his violin and played in the family parlour.

In his book *Souvenirs d'un peintre de montagne*, Albert Gos describes how, during his stays in Zermatt, he made friends with the children in the small hamlet of Blatten. "As I often sketched in that area the children would come and watch me paint. They were amazed. Little by little the conversation, at first halting, became amicable... I had bought some little objects at the bazaar in Zermatt, then some bonbons, oranges, chocolate and a large white brioche. What a change from their black bread!" He remembers, too, the enthusiasm of the children and the gratitude of the grown-ups when one evening he brought his violin to Blatten and gave a concert for his new friends.[11]

"In Zermatt the women, old people and children seem to carry the main responsibility for cultivating the fields. Even the arduous harvesting of fodder appears to be their task."
Alfred Ceresole, 1894

Except for the painter's gifts, Ulrich and his sisters and brothers possessed no toys, neither a ball for the summer nor a sledge for the winter.

The painter Albert Gos

They played instead with pieces of wood or bones that in their imagination took the shapes of animals. With twigs the children built fences and stalls for the animals, and with stones they built walls. But most of their childhood was occupied with work; there was little time for amusement.

Children in Hinterdorf, a part of Zermatt. The older ones take care of their younger siblings.

As soon as children were big enough to take on some task they had to help their parents. Even at the age of four, Ulrich looked after his younger siblings, brushed the cows and gathered firewood and litter for the cowsheds.

In spring, when the snow had melted, the children went daily into the Aroleit wood near Blatten to collect larch needles which had fallen from the trees in autumn. The needles, called "chris", were then strewn in the cowsheds. Straw was too precious for this purpose: it was cut very short and mixed with hay for fodder. Since large quantities of litter were needed in winter, Ulrich and his brothers and sisters spent a considerable time collecting "chris", preferably under a rising moon, which was supposed to exert a favourable influence. The children raked the larch needles together, piled them under trees like anthills and covered them with branches. After the first snowfall their father transported the humus-like mass by sledge to the cowshed in Zermatt while the children took enough for immediate needs directly to the cowshed in Blatten.

Another job for the children was gathering firewood. In the municipal area of Zermatt the inhabitants were allowed to collect only wood that was lying on the ground, or they could dig out stumps. It was strictly forbidden to cut down trees. This ban was supposed to prevent deforestation and thereby reduce the danger from avalanches. But there were also other reasons. St. Kronig wrote in 1927: "A great deal of firewood was taken from the communal forests for the hotel industry. The only reason why Zermatt is now so short of wood is the construction of hotels and the amount of firewood used by them."[12]

Ulrich and his brothers and sisters hunted almost daily for fallen branches and twigs. Wherever they saw a piece of wood on the ground they would pick it up and carry it home. Ulrich cannot remember ever coming home without a branch or small piece of wood. He especially liked to watch when his father blew up the stump of a big larch tree with dynamite so that the deep roots could be dug up. The firewood for the winter was initially stored in the woods and later brought to the Haus Vispa by sledge.

When Ulrich was five years old one of his jobs was looking after the cows. He recalled later that he preferred tending cows to children. Mostly he was accompanied by Albinus or Martha. As early as around 7.30 in

Mit meiner Schwester Martha am
Wassertrog zwischen Zumsee + Blatten

With my sister Martha at the water trough between Zum See and Blatten

the morning the children took the animals to the pastures. When they went far from home their eldest sister Maria brought them lunch in a tin.

While watching the cows the children passed the time playing, but without letting the cows out of their sight. Supervising the animals was a responsible job, since each cow cost between 300 and 400 francs and thus represented a small fortune. The children had to see that the animals did not graze on meadows belonging to neighbours or on slopes that were too steep. The clanging of the cowbells helped them to fulfil their duty. Before the animals were led back to the cowshed in the evening for milking they had to be cleaned with a coarse brush.

In autumn Ulrich and Martha tethered the cows to stakes in the pastures, where their father had left some grass standing in a few places after the second hay harvest. When an area had been grazed the animals were moved a few metres further on. Ulrich and his siblings then adopted a very old practice they had learned from their parents. To fertilise the ground they spread out cow dung in circles with a broom or a pitch-fork. An account of these "mysterious" and often intertwined circles was given in a book about Zermatt by Henry Hoek: "As soon as the cows were unpegged the herdsman or herdswoman began to sweep wildly round in circles. The result was circles that were all of exactly the same size."

In July and September the family set out with bag and baggage on the hour-long walk from Blatten to Zmutt. The parents carried the small children and drove the cows. Ulrich and his two older sisters carried the cackling hens on their backs in baskets called "Tschiffra". Only the cat could not be packed; usually she followed a day later. Once, when she had three young ones, she turned up in Zmutt the day after the move with all her kittens. During the night she must have made the journey three times to fetch her offspring. On the way between Blatten and Zmutt the children often saw marmots, foxes, squirrels and vipers. Above Zmutt they also encountered chamois and ibex.

The Inderbinen family's residence was located at "Outer Mutt" (Äussere Mutt), a few minutes away from the actual hamlet where several families lived. The house consisted of two storeys with a kitchen and a parlour on the ground floor and a bedroom for Ulrich and his brothers in the attic. As in Blatten, there was neither electric light nor running water. Ulrich's mother fetched drinking water from a nearby trough fed by

"Olympic rings"

spring water, where she also washed the laundry before spreading it out on the grass to dry.

Behind the house there was a smooth rock that made a good slide for the children. In Zmutt they had many playmates, and their parents would also occasionally meet their neighbours in the evening for a companionable get-together.

Monika was the only child in the family to be born in this isolated hamlet. Since the midwife arrived in time the birth was trouble free, but the baptism was more difficult. Because of the high infant mortality newborns had to be baptised as quickly as possible. Therefore, only a few

Zmutt: der Pfeil zeigt auf unser Haus

Zmutt: the arrow points to our house.

hours after the birth, Hieronymus carried the new-born child down to the village, fetched the godparents and had Monika baptised. Then he had to hurry to get the very hungry baby back to its mother before darkness fell.

The hamlet of Zmutt was until 1791 an independent little village with its own jurisdiction.

View from our house (on the right) towards "Inner Mutt"

There were no forests in the immediate vicinity of Zmutt, so Ulrich and his brothers and sisters gathered wood and "chris" in the forest on the opposite side of the valley, which was separated from Zmutt by a deep, narrow gorge. The dizzy abyss was spanned by a ramshackle wooden bridge above the main hamlet called "Inner Mutt".

As they had done previously in Blatten the children carried home litter and firewood for daily use in baskets on their backs. Larch and pine needles and firewood for the winter were stored in piles in the shelter of the trees to await winter. Other families were also collecting for the winter so there were carefully stacked piles of "chris" and firewood everywhere, yet there was never any confusion over the ownership of the heaps.

In Zmutt, Ulrich and his brothers and sisters found a way of earning a little money. They searched for edelweiss and gave them away to tourists or led the visitors to places where rare alpine flowers grew. The 20 centimes they received without prompting were handed over to their mother.

Often thirsty travellers paused to rest in front of the Inderbinens' house, having looked in vain for a restaurant in the hamlet. Ulrich's mother would willingly offer them refreshment. For a cup of fresh milk they would sometimes express their thanks with photos (some of which appear in this book). After September tourists came only occasionally to Zmutt. In October, when the larch woods turned golden, the residents of the hamlet were again on their own.

My mother and one of my sisters with two tourists in front of our house in Zmutt

After the harvest had been gathered in the autumn, Ulrich's family remained in Outer Mutt until mid-December. Not until the cows had eaten the reserves of hay did they return to Zermatt. It would have been too much work to take the fodder all the way down to Zermatt and then, in the spring, carry the cow dung back up to the high meadows, where it was needed as manure.

> *"In school the pupil is obedient and alert... He avoids everything contrary to order and decorum, such as making a noise, eating, leaving his place without permission, unseemly attitudes etc."* The School Booklet

When Ulrich had to start school shortly before his eighth birthday, late autumn became the most difficult time for him. The school year in those days started at the beginning of November and lasted until the end of April. For Ulrich and his brothers and sisters this meant that for one and a half months they had to walk an hour from Zmutt to Zermatt and back again in the evening. Only in particularly bad weather, such as very heavy snowfalls and increased danger of avalanches, were the pupils from remote hamlets allowed to stay away from lessons and study at home.

The children rose at 6 a.m., had a meagre breakfast and set out in darkness on the long walk to school. Half way down they met up with their classmates from Furi and Zum See. Ulrich and Albinus carried schoolbooks, slates and slate pencils in wooden boxes with handles made by a carpenter. Maria had a school bag on her back which her mother had sewn together from remnants of cloth and leather. Snow often fell in November. When the narrow mountain track had been covered with snow during the night Albinus, being the eldest, had to go ahead to make a path for the others. Even after a short time the children had wet shoes and socks which they then had to wear for the rest of the day. They wore the same pair of nailed shoes day in day out, dry or wet, summer and winter, outside and inside the house.

The school day began with a half-hour Mass. After that the pupils went into one of the four classrooms in the village hall next to the church. The rooms on the south side of the building were heated by large stone stoves for which the pupils had to bring firewood. Since 1901 the primary school had consisted of two lower and two upper classes for boys and girls, who were taught separately. In each class there were pupils from four age groups because there were only four teachers. Ulrich's class numbered around 40 children, ten of whom were his age. Compulsory schooling lasted eight years but took up only six months of each year. There were strict rules on how pupils had to behave in and out of school. These were laid down in the School Booklet which each child received to enter his or her grades. The pupils were forbidden to:

"1. damage or write on the walls of the school room;
 2. answer back;
 3. use coarse or discourteous language;
 4. fight, swear or behave in a way that violates decency and decorum.

"Among themselves and in their personal relations pupils must be well-behaved, kind, obliging and courteous, never inciting anyone to be bad. Towards strangers they should be polite and helpful, never ridiculing old age or infirmity, careful not to besmirch doors or walls, not to become involved in fisticuffs, nor to be noisy, to smoke or to torment animals or destroy birds' nests. It is forbidden to steal fruit or damage trees or other people's property. Pupils who have the audacity to delete or alter grades in the School Booklet... will be penalised with a detention of from one to six days or with a fine of 5–30 francs."

The boys' classes were taught reading, writing, calligraphy, arithmetic, nature study and geography by teachers named Lehner and Bacher. The two girls' classes had additional instruction in housekeeping. They were taught by nuns of the order of St Ursula.

Lessons always started with a prayer. In all classes particular emphasis was placed on religious education, for which the priest, Johannes Bittel, was responsible. The emphasis was on learning the catechism by heart. Known as "Canisi" by the children, the catechism was by Peter Canesius, a severe Jesuit priest of the sixteenth century. The book was divided into questions and answers and began with the difficult question "Why are we here on Earth?".

My grandmother Aloysia lived on the second floor of the house on the left. The white building on the right is the Village Hall where I went to school.

Between midday and one o'clock Ulrich went with his brothers and sisters to have lunch with their grandmother Aloysia, who lived opposite the school. The children were usually very hungry, since only rarely had they been given a piece of bread for the school break. After Aloysia died in August 1911 the children spent the midday break in the unheated apartment in Haus Vispa. There, Ulrich's eldest sister Maria prepared a simple meal that mostly consisted of a milk soup and a little bread.

Death notice
of Ulrich's
grandmother

For pupils with a long way to go home the afternoon lessons lasted from 1–3.30 p.m.. Children who lived in the village had to remain in school until four o'clock. Before Ulrich left the classroom he crossed himself with holy water from a small stoop beside the door. Then, with his siblings, he walked back up to Zmutt. On the way there were several crucifixes at which the children crossed themselves and said a short prayer, as their parents had taught them, the boys respectfully taking off their hats. Whoever was in a hurry was permitted to replace a prayer with "good thoughts".

The children hurried past the "Bozugädini", cowsheds and sheep pens that were believed to be so horribly haunted that the owners had a Mass said every year to drive away evil. In contrast, there was no danger from the "Mäusestadel", or "mice barn", so called because only the front side stood on posts, so it was not protected from mice. When the "mice barn" came into view the children were only a few minutes from home.

Zmutt was reached shortly before dark. Under the supervision of their father the children did their homework by the light of an oil lamp. The curriculum was extensive. In Zermatt's short school year they had to learn the same material as was covered by pupils in other places who attended school for eight or nine months in the year.

"Canisi"

The Fourth Commandment of God

"Honour thy father and thy mother."

1. What doth God command in the Fourth Commandment?

He commandeth that children honour, love and obey their parents, and that subordinates act likewise towards those in authority over them.

2. Why should children obey, love and honour their parents?

Because parents are, after God, their greatest benefactors, being God's deputies in relation to them.

3. In what manner do children sin against their duty to honour their parents?

They sin against their duty to honour their parents if they 1) scorn their parents in their hearts, 2) talk ill of their parents, 3) behave coarsely or defiantly towards them.

"The eye that mocketh at his father and that despiseth the labour of his mother in bearing him, let the ravens of the brooks pick it out, and the young eagles eat it." Proverbs 30,17.

4. In what manner do children sin against the love they owe their parents?

They do sin against love they owe their parents if they 1) do not pray for their parents, 2) make them sorrowful and wrathful, 3) do not stand by them in time of need, 4) do not bear their infirmities with fortitude.

"He that striketh his father or mother, shall be put to death." Exodus 21,15.17. "Son, support the old age of thy father and grieve him not in his life." Ecclesiasticus 3,14. Example: Jesus who, dying on the cross, still cared for his mother.

5. How do children sin against the duty of obedience?

They sin against the duty of obedience if they 1) obey their parents grudgingly or not at all, 2) do not lend willing ears to their warnings, 3) resist punishment from them.

"If a man have a stubborn and unruly son, who will not hear the commandments of his father or mother, and being corrected slighteth obedience... the people of the city shall stone him: and he shall die... and all Israel hearing it may be afraid." Deuteronomy 21,18.21.

6. What must children expect who do not fulfil their duties to their parents?

In this life the curse of God, shame and ignominy; in the next life eternal damnation.

"Cursed be he that honoureth not his father and mother. And all the people shall say: Amen." Deuteronomy 27,16. "Remember thy father and thy mother: for thou sittest in the midst of great men. Lest God forget thee in their sight and thou.. wish that thou hadst not been born, and curse the day of thy nativity." Ecclesiasticus 23,18.19. Examples: Ham, Absalon and the sons of the high priest Eli.

7. What may children expect who faithfully obey the Fourth Commandment?

In this life God's protection and blessing, in the next eternal salvation.

"Honour thy father and thy mother, which is the first commandment with a promise; that it may be well with thee, and thou mayest be long lived upon earth." Ephesians 6,2.3. Examples: Shem, Isaac, the young Tobias.

8. Who besides our parents are our superiors to whom we owe honour, love and obedience?

Foster parents, teachers, masters [of apprentices], people of rank, and all our spiritual and temporal superiors.

9. How must one behave towards foster parents, teachers and masters?

One must regard them as deputies and assistants of parents and therefore accord them in due proportion what children owe their parents.

10. How do servants sin against their masters?

By disobedient or surly behaviour, 2) by indolence, unfaithfulness, 3) most of all when they lead astray the children of the house into wickedness.

"Servants, obey in all things your masters according to the flesh, not serving to the eye, as pleasing men, but in simplicity of heart, fearing God." Colossians 3,22. "Servants, be subject to your masters with all fear, not only to the good and gentle but also to the froward." I Peter 2,18.

11. How does one sin against spiritual and temporal authority?

1) By contempt, 2) by impudent criticism and blasphemy, 3) by insubordination and insurrection, 4) if one does not pay the customary or obligatory taxes.

"With all thy soul fear the Lord, and reverence his priests." Ecclesiasticus 7,31. "Let every soul be subject to higher powers: for there is no power but from God: and those that are, are ordained of God. Therefore he that resisteth the power, resisteth the ordinance of God. And they that resist, purchase to themselves damnation." Romans 13,1.2.

After the evening meal everyone said the rosary together. Then, before going early to bed, each child would say the evening prayer:
"To thee, O God, my heart I lift, and thank you for your every gift. And if you are with me displeased, I ask you to forgive me, please."

"The lonely village, enclosed by white walls, sees the snow grow deeper every day, covering it with a blanket that muffles every sound and drives life into the interiors of the black huts."
François Gos, 1925

Shortly before Christmas every year, life would become simpler for Ulrich and his siblings because they would move to the apartment on the first floor of the Haus Vispa, close to the school. This saved them the wearisome walk down to the village. Ulrich remembers that the Inderbinens were the last family to leave Zmutt, so they would "close the hamlet down". The other inhabitants had already left a few weeks before. On the day of the move Hieronymus would heat the house thoroughly for one last time so that "poor souls" could warm themselves in winter.

This fifth and last move of the year was the most difficult. By the middle of December there was usually a lot of snow on the ground. Hieronymus and Maria Inderbinen made the journey twice, first to take the animals down, then the children and heavily laden sledges. To prevent the cows slipping on the icy path Hieronymus would first shovel snow over dangerous patches.

Their winter accommodation in Haus Vispa was spacious compared with their two other residences. It consisted of a kitchen, a large room and a small room. The furnishings were plain and functional: a cooking stove, table and chairs in the kitchen; a stone stove and beds for the parents and the younger children in the large room; beds for the older children in the small room. There were no armchairs or settees. The kitchen was lit by an oil lamp until the 1920s, and in the two other rooms the electric lighting was used only sparingly.

Parents and children washed themselves in the basin in the kitchen, which had had running water since 1907. The icy water was warmed in a

Haus Vispa in winter. On the left is the former slaughterhouse.

bowl that could be placed in a recess at the back of the kitchen stove. The beautiful stone stove in the living room was used only rarely but mother kept the kitchen stove burning day and night, and it provided some warmth for the other rooms too.

In the first few days after the move from Zmutt to Zermatt the apartment was still cold and cheerless. The small room which Ulrich shared with his older brother and two sisters was sometimes so chilly that the snow which had fallen from their shoes in the evening lay unmelted on the same spot the following morning.

As in Blatten and Zmutt, all eleven members of the family slept in double bunk beds, two in upper beds and two in lower "drawer" beds which were pulled out in the evening. In the Haus Vispa there were proper mattresses but in their summer quarters children and parents lay on straw-filled bags which were covered with linen sheets. For bedspreads, they used woollen blankets woven by the mother.

By the time the Inderbinen family moved into their Zermatt dwelling the village had been in hibernation for two months. Before the introduction of winter services on the Visp–Zermatt railway in 1929 the villagers lived from October to May much as they had done in the old days described by Emil Yung in his book *Zermatt and the Visp Valley* published in 1893: "In winter the inhabitants of Zermatt hardly ever leave the cosy nook by the open fire in their kitchens, and only venture outdoors to feed the cows and sheep which spend the winter in widely scattered stables... On the whole their lives are not unlike those of their friends the marmots".

In 1905, Guido Rey gave this account of the end of the summer season: "The shopkeepers pack up their merchandise, the musicians take their instruments under their arms... the hotels close down; for eight months Zermatt sleeps and dreams of the time when it was peaceful little 'Praborgne' [the name by which Zermatt was known in the early thirteenth century]".

For some visitors, however, winter in Zermatt was magical. Arnold Lunn wrote this just before the First World War: "Those who knew the old Zermatt are unpleasantly fond of reminding us that the railway train and the monster hotels have robbed Zermatt of its charm; while the fixed ropes and sardine tins... have finally humiliated the unvanquished Titan. It may be so; but it is easy enough to recover the old atmosphere. You have only to visit Zermatt in winter when the train is not running. A long trudge up the twenty miles of shadowed, frosty valley and a little bluff near Randa, and the Matterhorn soars once more into a stainless sky. There are no clouds, and probably not another stranger in the valley. The hotels are closed, the sardine cans are buried, and the Matterhorn renews like the immortals an undying youth."[14]

For the villagers winter was less romantic. Contact with the outside world was maintained only by the mule post which came twice a day. The mule driver had a hazardous occupation because the entire Visp valley, especially the stretch between Zermatt and Täsch, was exposed to

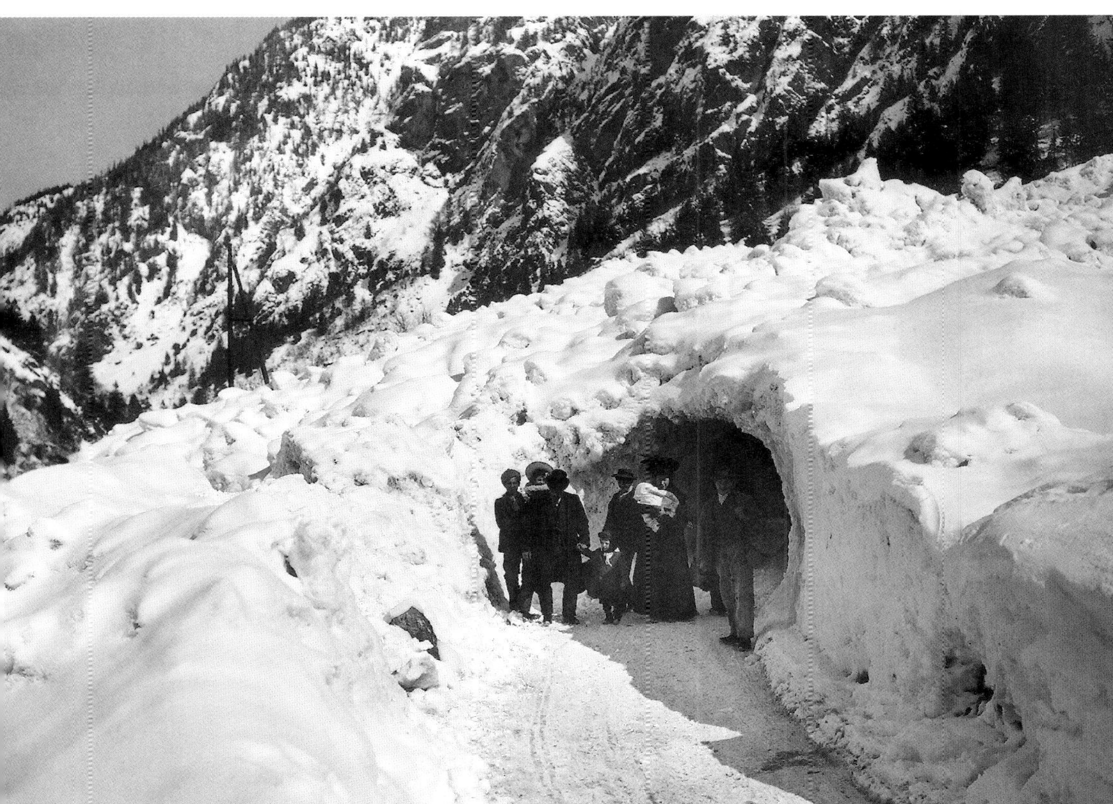

Tunnel through an avalanche

avalanches. The church bells tolled often to summon the men of the village to clear an avalanche. When it was a big one, a tunnel was dug through the mass of snow. In March 1904 one such tunnel reached a length of 300 metres (*Journal de Zermatt*, 1904). But the village streets were not cleared, so there were only narrow paths bordered by high walls of snow. When the children met adults coming the other way they were expected to step aside to make way for them.

Winter sports were rare at the beginning of the century, and skiing did not become known in Zermatt until 1898. There were few skis and no pistes.[15] Some children made oval snow shoes from barrel staves; others

Zermatt. The guardian angel was watching. Two little girls, sweet blondes of 5–6 years old, disport themselves sledging near the village, not far from the River Vispa. They are the daughters of the mountain guides Aloys Biner and Adolf Schaller. Suddenly the sledge slides out over the ice of the partly frozen river. Schaller's little girl falls from the sledge and remains lying on the ice. The other little girl shoots straight out into the water. A piercing cry of "Mama! Mama!" rends the air; then the rosy lips are silent. The evil waterman grabs the poor little creature and her sledge and sweeps her down the valley in his powerful current. For 20 metres he clutches her in his wet arms. But the guardian angel is watching. As if by chance, the worthy priest arrives on scene at the moment of the catastrophe. He leaps into the water. Before the poor child disappears under the ice he grabs her and becomes her rescuer.

My guardian angel, look after me!

L. Th.

In February 1908 there was an accident in front of the Haus Vispa involving two children of Ulrich's neighbours.

Briger Anzeiger, February 1908

carved skis from larch or ash wood and attached simple bindings to take their nailed boots. These skis were for walking rather than skiing. During his eight years at school Ulrich went skiing with his class only two or three times. He had to borrow the skis because his home-made snow shoes were not suitable for downhill runs. He still remembers well the occasion when he had to abandon a school ski race from Furi to Zermatt because his loose bindings fell apart.

Only a few days after the move from Zmutt the Inderbinen family celebrated Christmas in the village. On Christmas Eve a decorated Christmas tree stood in the living room and the stone stove burned vigorously. There was a specially sumptuous meal. Apples and nuts were handed out as presents and knitted clothes from their mother. As a rule only practical things were given as presents; if the children needed new shoes they received them as a present at Christmas. The parents could not buy sweets or toys for nine children. They lived frugally so as to ride out the long winter without worrying. When the harvest was bad they had to buy more food, and savings were quickly used up.

Feeding and educating the eleven-member family was costly. How hard it was for parents to send several children to school at the same time is revealed in an article headed "The Burden of Schooling!" in the *Walliser Bote* of 1 November 1916: "School gives the head of a poor family much worry. It is no small matter for him to send half a dozen children to school at the same time. First of all he must, of course, provide somewhat better clothing than they would normally wear. Then he has to buy all the school materials, which nowadays weigh almost more than the child. That costs money, but where is it to be found?".

For Ulrich and his siblings winter meant school. The short days were taken up with lessons and homework. After 4.30 p.m. schoolchildren were forbidden to leave their houses. Any who were caught in the street by a teacher or the priest were punished by having to copy a chapter from the Catechism. The favourite was the Fourth Commandment because the three-page section on "Honour thy father and thy mother" also contained the obligation to honour, love and obey teachers. To avoid punishment Ulrich did not play in the street except on Thursdays, when there was no school. Like the other children he was afraid the priest might be standing in the church tower looking out for offenders.

The fountain in the Hinterdorf quarter of Zermatt where my mother did the washing in winter

Mutter im Winter die Wäsche

From a Catholic catechism

On days when there was no school, the children helped their parents tend the livestock. The cows, which spent the winter in a cowshed behind Haus Vispa, had to be fed, watered and cleaned, and their stalls mucked out. Only for the milking, morning and evening, was mother solely responsible. Maria Inderbinen spent a lot of time in winter darning, knitting, sewing clothes with an old sewing machine and spinning wool for her large family. From the wool she wove not only pullovers, socks and gloves but also blankets. A loom was available for all the women of the village in a house next to the church square.

In winter father repaired the living quarters, cowsheds, barns and store-rooms. Almost daily he went into the forest with a sledge to fetch "chris" and firewood from the piles that had been stored there. To slow down the sledge he constructed a simple brake with a tree trunk tied on with a rope and dragged behind. In Zermatt he took the "chris" to the cowshed and then sawed, split and stacked the wood at the Haus Vispa. In the evenings he supervised his children's homework. He also cut their hair, preferably when the moon was rising because he believed it made for healthy hair.

When he had time, Hieronymus used larchwood and flexible sticks to construct the baskets, known as "Tschiffra", that were carried on the back like rucksacks. The boys helped him scrape the bark off the branches with knifes. Only very occasionally did Ulrich's father go for a few hours to the "club", a heated room in the village hall in which the local men met to play cards. He practically never allowed himself a visit to the tavern. He seems to have been untypical in working so hard. The famous Zermatt hairdresser Marie Biner, who also cut Edward Whymper's hair,

74

was once asked by a guest what the men of the village did in winter, since the women looked after the cattle. "She replied that in good weather they lie around on the tables and wait for midday, and in the afternoons they hang around until the sun sets."[16]

The children could hardly wait for spring and the end of the school year. On the last day of school there was spring cleaning. In the school yard the pupils zealously scrubbed the desks and benches. When a brush could not do the job they used sandpaper and glass splinters to remove ink from the woodwork.

When reports were distributed the best pupils were rewarded with a missal, the less good with a small picture of a saint. Ulrich, although he describes himself as a poor pupil, "born stupid and learnt nothing", had the pleasure of receiving a missal at the end of his first year at school.

After completing his third year he took his first communion wearing his Sunday clothes with a white stole over his right arm. From then on he had to go to confession once a month and take it in turns with his school-mates to be an altar boy.

With the end of the school year the Inderbinen family set out again on its wanderings.

> *"We see others working on their knees in the fields, struggling with the sweat of their brows to extract their nourishment from Mother Earth, who is here such a poor provider..."*
>
> Emil Yung, 1896

When Ulrich was ten his younger brothers and sisters took over his duties so he could help his parents in the fields. As soon as the snow melted, he and Albinus cleared the fields in the avalanche slopes of stones and branches left behind from the winter. Next they checked the water courses which irrigated the pastures. The hundred-year-old conduits, which were man-made ditches partly of wood, had to be cleaned out and repaired. When they had finished this work the boys transported cow dung in "Tschiffras" to the pastures, reduced it to small pieces and spread it out

For my first communion I still went to the old church. In the foreground the garden of the Hotel Zermatterhof.

76

Im Vordergrund der Garten des Hotels Zermatterhof 1906

with pitchforks. After a few days, when the dung was dry, they swept it together again, gathered it up, took it to the corn fields and spread it out once more. In shaded areas they first spread ashes so that the snow would melt more quickly. The same work had to be carried out a few weeks later on the higher lying pastures and fields of Zmutt. In June, with their mother and sisters, the boys also planted vegetable and potato seedlings.

From the beginning of June to the end of August it was Ulrich's job to water the pastures daily. The local authority allocated each family times when it was allowed to take water. The water was then diverted with an iron plate into their own ditch that was dammed so that it overflowed and flooded the pasture. It was particularly difficult to water sloping fields in this way. Ulrich had to keep shifting the iron plate a few metres to achieve an even distribution of water. Every few weeks the small irrigation ditches had to be maintained.

The rewards of this work were to be seen within a short time in the form of abundant flowers and lush pastures, the origins of which were the subject of a legend about Zermatt:
"Once upon a time, when the valley lay desolate and abandoned, the wind brought a cloud of seeds which, on their long, airy journey, had flown through a rainbow before descending to earth. They germinated in the alien soil, and, lo and behold, the flowers bloomed in the thousand hues of the rainbow through which they had passed."

Haymaking started at the beginning of July, first in the low-lying meadows, then in Blatten and Herbrigg, and finally in Zmutt and its surrounding area. By six o'clock in the morning, when the church bells rang for the first Mass, Ulrich and his family were already in the fields. As they heard the bells they stopped work and said a short prayer. If weather conditions were unfavourable the priest could give them permission to harvest on Sundays.

When Ulrich and Albinus were strong enough to wield scythes they cut the long grass with their father. A day or two after cutting they turned the hay several times to dry, then raked it together, bundled it up and carried it on their heads to the nearest cowshed. There they had to haul the heavy bundles up a ladder and throw them through the door under the roof into the storeroom that lay below. In the heat of summer this was heavy work, especially for children.

In August it was time to harvest the "winter rye" which had been sown in the autumn of the previous year, leaving the seeds dormant over the winter. The grain harvest was difficult. The stony ground mostly sloped steeply, and every square metre was exploited. Small stone walls, built many generations before, prevented landslides. Hieronymus and his sons began work on the rye fields in the early morning when the grains of rye were still moist and would not fall out so easily. First they cut the crop with sickles, then they bundled it up carefully, so that no grain was lost, wrapped it in a two-metre square "fodder cloth" and carried it on their heads to the nearest granary, where it was stored. If there was enough room the bundles were placed upright.

Children carrying the "Tschiffra" in the "Hinterdorf"

At the beginning of September the grass on the pastures was cut again. This second mowing was less productive, especially on the higher meadows, but it required the same amount of work as the first haymaking. In autumn Ulrich's father also went alone to Hohbalm, the alpine pastures above Zmutt, where he could cut wild hay on communal ground. Hieronymus did not take the children with him because the slopes were rocky and prone to landslides. He left the short wild hay to dry for a few days and then carried it down the steep mountainside in a cloth.

In September the harvested rye fields were turned over. Hieronymus sowed new rye – the "sleeping corn" – while the boys dug over the furrows. At the end of the summer the potatoes were also harvested and stored in the cellar with carrots, leeks, white cabbages and turnips. Finally, in October, the boys had once more to take manure to the fields.

Only after this work was finished did Ulrich go back to the various granaries with his father and brother. In each barn there was a corridor between the storage rooms in which the ears of corn were threshed with a flail to remove the grain. The children gathered up the grain and shook it in a flat basket that served as sieve to separate the corn from the chaff. After that they loaded the clean grain into baskets and carried the heavy loads on their backs to the cornmill in the village, where the rye was ground. The flour was put into bags, deposited in store rooms and later taken to the bakery as required. The communal bakery could be used by each family only on a specified day each month. For this reason a lot of bread was always baked in advance. Baking was man's work, so Ulrich helped his father. They had to bring their own wood to heat the oven. The finished rye bread was kept in a store-room on specially built shelves called "bread ladders" and lay there for several months, gradually becoming as hard as stone. Only with some force and a good knife could larger pieces be sawn off. These were then soaked in milk or soup.

"I earned my first pay as a shepherd."

In 1913, when Ulrich was a fully-fledged worker like his older brother, his father decided to buy a few sheep. He had just sold a piece of land in the centre of the village to the hotelier Alexander Seiler. From the pro-

Alexander Seiler with my father, little Medard and my sisters at our house in Blatten

ceeds he purchased a bigger, agriculturally productive piece of land on the outskirts of the village. The rest of the money was used to buy the sheep, which in those days cost 50–60 francs each. Soon the flock consisted of more than 30 animals, which were looked after by the two boys and their father.

Rechts unterhalb der Strasse das verkaufte

Grundstück

On the right, below the road, the piece of land that was sold

In spring and autumn the boys herded the sheep in Blatten and Zmutt. At the end of May the animals were taken to the barren pastures of Hohbalm, which extended to an altitude of 2,800 metres. There they were left on their own for the whole summer.

Only twice a month did Hieronymus visit the sheep and drive them down the steep hillside to the alpine meadows of Trift, 400 metres below. There they were driven into a pen, counted and fed with "Gläck" – a mixture of salt and flour – to guard against salt deficiency. Afterwards the animals were taken back to the alpine pastures.

Ulrich often accompanied his father on this work. At 4 a.m. they both got up and set out on the journey of several hours. There was a small mountain inn in Trift which was open in summer, but Ulrich never stopped there with his father. A visit to a restaurant was more than their finances would allow and was never contemplated. Both of them had some milk and bread with them which they consumed after the work was done.

At the end of September the sheep were brought down to the Zmutt stream below Blatten. There they were held by the horns and turned over in the water to be washed. The next day Hieronymus began the shearing. With the help of his sons he was able to shear up to 20 animals in a day. In this work, too, as when cutting his children's hair and gathering "chris", he took account of the rising moon because he believed it promoted new growth. Most of the raw wool was taken to a collecting point in the village and sold for little money. The rest was spun by Ulrich's mother.

In November a few sheep and sometimes a cow were slaughtered. The reserves of sausage and meat, air-dried in the loft of the storehouse, had to last the whole year. The hides were allowed to dry in the sun, then folded and sent by post to tanners in the valley. Out of the tanned leather the shoemaker in Zermatt made new shoes.

From autumn until the end of January the sheep remained in the sheds in Zmutt. While the family lived there, and if no snow had fallen, the animals were let out and watched over each day. After the move to Zermatt in mid-December Hieronymus returned to Zmutt every day along the avalanche-prone path to tend the sheep. He was firmly convinced that avalanches would descend only when he was not on the path.

Hinter der Brücke wurden unsere
Schafe gewaschen

Our sheep were washed behind this bridge.

Das Hotel Trift

The Hotel Trift

Unsere Schafe in Blatten.
Die Tiere gehören zu der im Wallis
heimischen Rasse der Schwarznasenschafe

Our sheep in Blatten. They are a type of black-nosed sheep local to the Valais.

"They do not come when one is there", he used to say. He was the only shepherd in the place who left his flock in the remote hamlet in winter. To protect it from illnesses and other hazards he hung in every stall a juniper branch that had been blessed in church on Palm Sunday.

At the end of January the hay finally ran short and the animals were brought to sheds in Zum See and Aroleit, where the fodder from lower pastures was stored. Here the sheep could be fed and watered twice daily as the distance was not as great and the shepherds organised a kind of neighbourhood mutual help scheme. In the mornings the men took turns to feed all the flocks. In the afternoon the owners themselves went to muck out the stalls, feed and water the animals again and prepare fodder for the following morning.

In February the sheep were washed in the icy stream under the bridge below Blatten and sheared again the next day. Despite the winter temperatures this procedure was necessary so that the sheep would have enough wool in May to survive the cold alpine nights on Hohbalm. In March and April, as soon as the sun had melted the snow in a few places, the flocks could be let out for a couple of hours each day. In May they were herded by the children and finally, at the end of the month, driven up to the alpine pastures.

As a 13-year-old Ulrich also looked after the sheep of a family with whom they were friends, thereby earning his first money: 20 centimes a day. Unfortunately he did not see the money because it was paid directly to his father, but as a reward for his work he was allowed 10 centimes to buy a few caramels.

"Zermatt suddenly became still and quiet at a time when it was normally lively." Tourist Bureau Report, 1914

The opening of the Lötschberg tunnel in July 1913 gave Zermatt a good start to the summer season of 1914. As in previous years, hotels and guest houses were fully booked. The Bahnhofstrasse bustled with activity and orchestras played in the afternoons in the gardens and salons of the big hotels. Zermatt now had 28 hotels and guest houses with a total of 2,320

Hôtels de Zermatt.

Grand Hôtel Mont-Cervin et Villa Margherita	
Hôtel Victoria et d'Angleterre.	Société des Hôtels Seiler.
Hôtel Mont-Rose	
Buffet de la Gare	
Hôtel Schweizerhof	
Hôtel National	Société d'Hôtels.
Hôtel Belle-Vue	
Hôtel Beau-Site	A. Gindraux.
Hôtel de Zermatt	
Hôtel de la Poste	Mathier et Gattlen.
Hôtel du Gornergrat	P. Aufdenblatten, père.
Hôtel-Pension Perren	H. Perren.
Hôtel-Pension Breithorn . . .	P. Aufdenblatten, fils.
Hôtel du Parc	M. Aufdenblatten.
Hôtel-Pension Morgenroth . .	J. Marti.
Pension Gornergorge-Villa . .	H. Connell, Mme.
Pension Waldesruhe	L. Perren.
Pension des Alpes	E. Lauber.
Pension Hermetje	V. Furrer.
Pension du Glacier	J. Kronig.
Pension du Trift	J. Welschen.
Pension Gandegg	Pre-L. Perren.
Pension Staffelalp	J.-M. Binner, Mme.
Pension Alpina	Julier, R., Mme.

Hôtels de Zermatt-Montagne.

Hôtel Riffelalp (alt. 2227m) . .	Société des Hôtels Seiler.
Hôtel Lac Noir (alt. 2589m) . .	
Hôtel Riffelberg (alt. 2569m) . .	A. Gindraux.
Kulm-Hôtel-Gornergrat (alt. 3136m.)	

Distance en heures des Villes ci-dessous à Zermatt

Alger	45 h.	Edimbourg	32 h.	Munich	18 h.
Berlin	28 h.	Florence	12 h.	Nice	19 h.
Bordeaux	23 h.	Gênes	9 h.	Paris	14 h.
Brême	25 h.	Hambourg	25 h.	Rome	18 h.
Bruxelles	20 h.	Lisbonne	50 h.	Stockholm	52 h.
Caire	131 h.	Londres	22 h.	St-Pétersbourg	59 h.
Christiania	56 h.	Madrid	39 h.	Venise	11 h.
Copenhague	36 h.	Marseille	18 h.	Vienne	28 h.
Dijon	10 h.	Milan	6 h.		

Advertisement, 1911

beds. As usual, more than 90% of the visitors came from England, Germany, the United States, France, Holland, Spain and other European countries. There were even regular visitors from Egypt who had not been deterred by the 131-hour journey (see advertising on page 90).

Then came a heavy blow. At the end of July 1914, at the height of the summer season, the First World War broke out. Foreign guests rushed home. Almost overnight the hotels emptied and were forced to close. Large numbers of employees who earned their living in the tourist industry were prematurely dismissed. Numerous workers were not from Zermatt. "Before the World War many people went to work in hotels where

Valais.

Zermatt. Our little village has suddenly become empty. The soldiers have gone forth. With our hearts deeply stirred we wished them luck. The tourists of all nations have left in the greatest haste. The crowds of foreigners have been reduced to 100 in Riffelalp and 200 in Zermatt, mostly English ladies. What a transformation within one week! In the year 1870 there was none of this haste and fear, this stockpiling of food, this disturbance, this rush on the banks. But our Swiss people are also moved by higher, purer feelings of neighbourly love. All our newspapers are discussing how best to cope with increasing hardship. Swiss solidarity keeps watch in wartime: one for all and all for one!. Our Swiss mountains are deeply peaceful; they do not allow their tranquil splendour to be disturbed by the frantic madness of mankind. They admonish us to stay calm, guarded by the soldiers of the reserves — mostly family men. Recently four men on guard duty were asked about their children. Each one confessed to having 11 children at home. These four men thus have 44 children. That shows us what duty is. These men went out to protect the frontiers with their habitual calm, which, however, embraces the spirit of quiet self-sacrifice. Our people solemnly put their hands together and pray silently to Heaven: God protect our militia and shield our dear Fatherland!

Walliser Bote, 1914

foreigners stayed, particularly to Zermatt. Some earned good money there and did well. From Törbel alone some hundred people sought work away from home. Of these, 20–40 or more worked in Zermatt in the summer."[17]

At the beginning of August Switzerland ordered general mobilisation. The newspapers published appeals to the Swiss people "to remain vigilant and industrious in these serious times and devote your energies to the fatherland".

Women were called upon to show solidarity: "Do not make it difficult for men to report for duty by complaining about measures that are absolutely necessary for the security of our country. Shoulder with courage and wisdom the burdens that war brings upon you. Be frugal in your housekeeping so that the country's stocks of food and coal will not be consumed too quickly. Take on work of all kinds that cannot now be done by men, especially farming." (*Walliser Bote,* August 1914).

At the beginning of the war basic foods were rationed and the local authority in Zermatt issued coupons. Cattle raising, farming and local production of food, which had been partly displaced by tourism, became once again highly important. All the work connected with it now had to be done by women and children because men of military age had been sent to guard the mountain passes.

At the end of July 1914, as every year at this time, Ulrich was living with his family in Blatten, where the hay and rye crops were harvested. His parents received little information about political events. Only the twice-weekly local paper, the *Walliser Bote,* to which Ulrich's father subscribed for four francs a year, reported regularly on the war.

On 1 August Hieronymus was ordered to report for military service in Zermatt's Church Square. Since he was by that time 48 and amongst the oldest men liable for service he was required only to do daytime duty as a sergeant of the guard in the village. This meant that he was no longer available for farming, so his work was taken over by his children and his wife, who gave birth to her eleventh child that year.

Apart from taking on these extra duties Ulrich and his family were not directly affected by the war. They produced much of their own food so they had enough for their own needs. Rationing meant only shortages of sugar and paraffin. Yet the absence of foreign tourists was felt even in the little hamlets. The few walkers who found their way to Blatten and Zmutt would greet the locals in Swiss dialect. Gone were the friendly "Good mornings" of the British, who had been so numerous in Zermatt that, as early as 1869, a special church had been built for them, dedicated to St. Peter.[18]

In the summer of the second year of the war, Ulrich and Albinus were often woken at 2 a.m. by their father. In the dark they went together to the fields to start work. On days when Hieronymus had to report for guard duty at 8 a.m. the brothers worked on. In the course of the day they were helped by Maria and Martha. Ten-year-old Franziska helped her mother in the house while Berta looked after the cows. Six-year-old Monika took care of Medard and Veronika, the two youngest of the family.

Albinus, Medard and I in Zmutt

Zermatt in the summer of 1915 looked a bleak place. One of the few British visitors that year, E. A. Broome, wrote in the *Alpine Journal:* "I myself was unfortunately the only English climber and representative of this Club visible to the naked eye... Zermatt in 1915 was a desert. Its busy street was empty. Its shops were shut. Half of its hotels were closed, and the other half more than half empty. The Zermatt–Visp and Gornergrat railways ran very few trains, and carried a very unremunerative number of passengers. Hardly anyone could be seen on mountain paths, no one on the peaks. The English churches both at Zermatt and the Riffelalp were not open at all, and as an anti-climax the curious breed of loafers who wander aimlessly about the village with a rope over one shoulder and an axe in one hand were conspicuous by their absence! The most pathetic spectacle of all was the sprinkling of dismal, unhappy-looking guides, most of whom had not had a single client up to the middle of August... Yes! one felt very melancholy about the poor guides, especially the older ones, whose second bad season it was. The younger men seemed less in evidence and a good many were serving in the Army, while others had found temporary employment in the lower valleys on railways, electrical engineering, and in agricultural and even occasional urban work. One of the best known and most enterprising of all the young guides was reported to have been making some extra dare-devil ascents with a Bavarian, who had soon afterwards gone off his head and been taken to an asylum, to which place the said guide was invited, of course in the capacity of attendant to take charge of his Herr, and had then and there settled down with great success, 'as if a native and to the manner born'. After all, the difference between mountaineers and lunatics is not great..."[19]

A Swiss tourist took a more cheerful view of Zermatt: "For us... this time in Zermatt was a particularly rare and refined pleasure. Without the distraction of the lively, chattering groups of all nationalities that one normally encounters on every path it seemed to us, in those quiet summer days of the war, that the Matterhorn 'pyramid' conveyed its greetings to the valley more clearly, quietly and openly than in times of lively tourist activity."[20]

Only a few Swiss tourists were to be found in the village. The railways and the few hotels that were open suffered heavy losses. The Gornergrat

Railway carried only 6,000 passengers that summer, about a seventh of the normal number. In spite of reduced services it could not cover its costs. The same applied to the Visp–Zermatt Railway. Although it carried 20,000 passengers, this was only a fifth of the average pre-war number, and the high price of coal greatly increased costs.

With no end to the war in sight the locals became very worried about the future. Even the mountain farmers who depended only on the weath-

With my brothers and sisters in front of our house in Zmutt

er, not on tourism, lived more economically than before. If the harvest was poor they would have to buy rationed food for their families, and this had become much more expensive. For instance, the price of a kilo of potatoes had risen over a short period from 12 to 23 centimes.

When medical insurance came to Zermatt in the autumn of 1915 Hieronymus pondered long over whether it would be sensible to join while the war was on. In the end he decided against the additional expenditure, feeling that in such uncertain times he could not afford the annual subscription of 2–3 francs per person. Even a vivid newspaper article could not persuade him of the need for medical insurance.

Ulrich's final school year began in October. Once again he had to undertake the arduous walk to school and tackle the multitude of subjects in the curriculum. Beyond that lay the prospect of joining his parents and older siblings in agriculture. Any further education was out of the question because there was not enough money to pay for it. However, the war had shown that farming, in spite of its hardships, was a branch of the economy relatively unaffected by crises.

In the spring of 1916 Ulrich successfully completed his eight years of compulsory schooling. Together with the other boys in his class he was sent to St Niklaus to take the final examination. This was the first time he had been away from home. Girls were spared the trip because the examination was regarded as superfluous to their needs. The railway had not yet started its summer service so Ulrich and his classmates had to walk more than eleven miles down the valley to St Niklaus. They embarked on the trip with mixed feelings as they thought of the ordeal that lay ahead, but, after the written and oral exams, they strode home to Zermatt with lighter hearts.

Ulrich passed the exam but every week for several more years he had to squeeze himself behind a school desk for religious instruction. This was obligatory for school leavers. Boys and girls, taught separately, were made to learn the catechism and church history. They also had to attend "repeat classes" in winter, instituted in order to prevent them forgetting what they had learnt in school.

As usual, Ulrich spent the summer in Blatten and Zmutt, far from the empty hotels and unemployed guides of Zermatt. With his mother and siblings he worked in the fields, moving from one area to another. His father's tasks he shared with Albinus. Every other Saturday he rose early, packed some "Gläck" for the sheep, a piece of bread and a bottle of milk in his rucksack and climbed before dawn to Hohbalm. There he counted the sheep and fed them with the mixture of flour and salt before starting the long descent home. Around midday, eight hours after starting, Ulrich would reach the hamlet and work in the fields until evening, going to bed exhausted. He looked forward to Sundays but even then he could not sleep late because the family would leave together at 8 o'clock to attend High Mass in Zermatt. In August, when the parish acquired a new priest, Hieronymus, Maria and their children attended the festivities held for the new dignitary.

Walliser Bote,
August 1916

In November of the third year of the war Ulrich was allowed to accompany his father and Albinus to the "Martini" market in Visp. Beyond St Niklaus was new territory for Ulrich. The small mule track took them past the hamlet of Kalpetran, behind which rose cliffs so steep that local people used to joke that the chickens there climbed out of their eggs with crampons on their feet. Only a few kilometres further on the landscape changed. At Stalden the narrow valley widened, revealing open country, autumnal trees and vineyards. The village had a southern atmosphere. Vines adorned the houses, and a street in the middle of the village had been transformed into a skittle alley where the villagers gathered in the evening.

In the small town of Visp there were also many interesting things to see. Above all Ulrich was amazed by the bicycles and cars; although the street scene was still dominated by horse-drawn vehicles – in those days scarcely more than 20 cars were registered in the whole canton of Valais. Signs saying "Trotting prohibited. Penalty 3fr." ensured that traffic was regulated. For cars there was a maximum speed of 8 m.p.h.

In the cattle market Ulrich and Albinus watched the dealers in long black coats, and were impressed to see that some of them had pockets full of gold coins. When buying an animal it was usual to make a down payment with a gold coin worth about 20 francs, the deal being confirmed with the dialect name for the coin, *Kapara.* The war had pushed prices significantly higher than the previous year, and a cow now cost up to 700 francs.

Market Report. Visp, 13 November 1916.

Animals	totals	sold	price range in francs	
Horses	3	1	—	—
Breeding bulls	69	45	280	800
Oxen	50	26	380	880
Cows	182	90	400	700
Heifers	161	110	100	900
Calves	72	50	70	320
Pigs	24	9	15	180
Piglets	85	85	10	25
Sheep	316	77	25	100
Goats	96	32	40	58
Turnover: Good				

Walliser Bote

Hieronymus bought a sheep in Visp, so he and his sons could not cover the 22 miles back to Zermatt in one day. They therefore spent a night with acquaintances in St Niklaus. After their return the long, monotonous winter set in. Albinus left Zermatt to earn money elsewhere, and Ulrich was given new tasks by his father. Every day he had to go to Zmutt to tend the sheep. It took him five or six hours to make the journey there and back, feed and water the animals (of which there were now 60), clean out the stalls and spread new litter.

December began with heavy snowfalls which made his new duties even harder. Several metres of snow blocked the narrow path to Zmutt. Because of the high risk of avalanches Ulrich, who was just 16, had to wait three days before he could get through to the sheep. With wooden planks on their feet, he and his father then made a track through the snow, taking several hours to reach the snowed-in sheepsheds. Then they shovelled free the doors of the stalls and fed and watered the hungry and thirsty animals. As darkness fell they made their way home to Zermatt, arriving exhausted in the late evening.

Walliser Bote,
13 December 1916

A welcome change in the second half of winter was the carnival in February, when the young people of the village made merry from Sunday to the eve of Ash Wednesday in the large, unheated hall of the Hôtel des Alpes. This ball was the only occasion in winter when the villagers could dance. Local musicians played on the violin, trumpet, clarinet and dulcimer. There was cake and wine, and anyone who had a carnival costume would wear it. Ulrich, who as a schoolboy had been denied amusement of any sort, was at last able to take part in the festivities. Lacking a costume, he wore his jacket inside out.

The war was hardly noticeable in winter. Only the regular arrival of Italian deserters over the Theodul Pass reminded local people of world events. In February 1917 the *Walliser Bote* reported from Zermatt: "On the 19th of this month an Italian deserter arrived, and the next day another. The last was accompanied by two guides and two women whose husbands are already in Switzerland. The two female deserters were in a good mood and sang as they came down the mountain. They said they had to suffer many shortages at home, particularly of salt."

There was still no sign of an end to the war. As the villagers had feared, the fourth summer of the conflict again brought only Swiss tourists to Zermatt. "A large proportion of the best local talent stood idly at the station and in the street. Of the 50 or so guides who remained in the village, in spite of the war, only a few could find work; the others took their

leisure with their pipes in their mouths while their wives toiled at home."
(*Alpina,* 1917)

The railways, hotels and shops suffered another year of losses. Once again the season had to end prematurely. The disappointment was expressed by the *Walliser Bote* of 17 September: "With the fine September weather the end of the season has arrived. Almost unbelievable? What has this summer brought us? Mainly 62 Italian refugees in July and August. We could have done with more tourists...".

But the worst was yet to come. The following year an influenza epidemic swept Europe, putting a stop to all summer tourist traffic in Zermatt. In the Valais alone 1,500 people died from the effects of the disease. In Zermatt many villagers fell ill. Within a few weeks 22 died. The catastrophic effect on the tourist traffic is revealed in the statistics of the Gornergrat Railway. In the summer of 1918 it carried only 3,713 passengers – 10% of the total in 1899.

The Inderbinen family was not hit by the epidemic because, as usual, they spent most of the year in Blatten and Zmutt. But the children listened anxiously as the bells tolled regularly in the village below to announce another death: three times for a man, twice for a women. Hieronymus, who had already lost six children, prayed for the health of his family. In the autumn the situation improved and the long-awaited end of the war allowed hopes to rise for a better future.

The year brought Ulrich a crucial new experience. That winter, still just under 18 years old, he left his family for the first time to look for work elsewhere, as his brother Albinus had done before him. In October, with eight other men from the village, he walked down to Visp and boarded a train to St Maurice, where they were to work on military fortifications. He was the youngest on the building site. Six days a week he worked 10 hours a day for 90 centimes an hour. Evenings he spent in the dormitory huts playing cards with his colleagues from Zermatt. Except for High Mass on Sundays there was no break in the monotony, so winter in the dreary town of St Maurice seemed endless. For six months Ulrich was separated from his parents, brothers and sisters. Since the Visp–Zermatt train was at that time still closed in winter he could not go home on Sundays and holidays. He greatly missed the familiar security of his family, especially on his birthday and at Christmas.

Eventually spring arrived. At the end of April Ulrich returned to Zermatt with the first money he had ever earned apart from the few centimes as a shepherd boy – six months' wages amounting to nearly 1500 francs. Proudly he handed it over to his parents. He was immensely happy to be home. Even the hardest labour in the fields was better than working on the building site. Shortly after his return he accompanied his father to Stalden to buy a piglet. Stowing it in the "Tschiffra", he walked more than 17 miles home with the struggling animal on his back.

After toiling hard through the summer of 1919, Ulrich and Albinus had once again to say goodbye to their family and earn money elsewhere. As in the previous year, Hieronymus could not find work for both his boys in the same place. Ulrich went with a group of twelve villagers to the canton of Uri, where workers were needed to build a tunnel from Gurtnellen to Amsteg. He was allocated to the smithy, for which he had to fetch damaged drills from the tunnel and repair them. This work had the great advantage that Ulrich spent very little time in the tunnel. Many of his colleagues who had to work underground all the time became ill with silicosis, the so-called "dusty lung", because at that time boring was done without water, which was later used to keep the dust down. After five months Ulrich returned home just in time to till the fields.

In the summer of 1920 the number of tourists rose sharply. For the first time since the outbreak of war there were more foreign visitors, especially British and Dutch. The Visp–Zermatt railway carried 47,000 passengers, not quite as many as in the year of Ulrich's birth but the trend was showing a distinct turn for the better.

For the Inderbinen family, who still lived independently of tourism, life became progressively easier. All the children could now help in the fields. The youngest son, Medard, was nine years old, the youngest daughter, Veronika, six. A family picture taken in 1920 shows Hieronymus and Maria sitting contentedly surrounded by their children. Albinus was made to stand at the side so as to show his fine socks, knitted by his mother. Little Medard, on the other hand, was told to hide the holes in his shoes by kneeling on the ground with his feet behind him.

In October Ulrich had to report to St Niklaus for a military aptitude test. As the train was still running that autumn, he and the other men of his age decided to let the army pay for them to use it. This was Ulrich's

The Inderbinen family around 1920: in the front row, Medard, my father, Monika, my mother, Veronika and Bertha. Behind them: Albinus, Martha, myself, Maria and Franziska.

first experience of the Visp–Zermatt train, as it was for most of his colleagues. When the steam locomotive swayed into motion, gathering speed towards its maximum of 9 m.p.h., the future soldiers soon felt so sick that they spent the rest of the trip on the running board outside the carriage.

At the recruiting station, in spite of the pale face that he had acquired through travel sickness, Ulrich was found fit for military service and put down for training school in the coming April. At his own request he was allocated to the mountain infantry, a branch of the army that was also preferred by his colleagues. All the men of Zermatt agreed that there was one job they did not want, and that was mule driver responsible for transporting materials by mule. One of Ulrich's friends, a large, strong man whom the recruiting commission proposed as muleteer, offered a plausible explanation: "We Zermatters have already spent far too much time with these wretched animals."

On the train ride back to Zermatt the young men avoided the risk of being sick again by immediately climbing on the outside step for the one-hour trip.

Until April Ulrich could find no work outside Zermatt, so, to his great joy, he spent the winter at home. For 20 francs he bought his first skis made of larch wood. With their impressive length of 2.2 metres they reached more than half a metre above his head, while his hazelwood ski sticks rose above his shoulders. When he had to tend the sheep in Zmutt he took his skis with him and cruised happily home across the meadows. His free time was spent playing cards with friends.

On Christmas Eve he went to church with his colleagues to help the sacristan ring the bells continuously from 9 p.m. to midnight. At other times the sacristan did the job alone: "The bellringer of the new church in Zermatt has the reputation of being a virtuoso. He is able to ring all four bells on his own by sitting enthroned on a high seat and pulling the four ropes with his hands and feet. Using this method, however, the bells cannot resonate properly but instead give out a peculiar staccato sound with a distinct rhythm" (*Alpina,* 1916). The young men of Zermatt loved ringing the bells on Christmas because they were paid with meat and wine.

In the spring of 1921 Ulrich went through eight weeks of basic military training in Thun, where he received a pair of new nailed boots with five pages of instructions on how to care for them. For the first time he saw a lake, the Thunersee, but it did nothing for his confidence because he had never had a chance to learn to swim.

Exchanging thoughts with men of his age in Thun made Ulrich consider his future. For some time he and Albinus had been thinking of following a different career from their father. If they were to make a living and raise families in Zermatt the alternatives were limited to the hotel industry or mountain guiding. For them the choice was not difficult. Hotels and restaurants did not attract them. In any case, a full-time job in summer would conflict with their duties on their father's farm. Mountain guides, in contrast, enjoyed a certain independence, while the steady increase in visitors since the end of the war held out the prospect of good earnings.

The registered guide was a relatively recent innovation, brought in to replace the smugglers, dubious roving "shepherds" and others who used to guide unwary travellers across the mountain passes. The Zermatt guides quickly acquired a reputation for skill and courage. "They are a sturdy race, those Zermatt valley guides. One feels that they are capable of the most bold and risky enterprises. Many have a world-wide reputation..."[21]

"In the club huts of Canada names such as Inderbinen are mentioned only with the greatest respect." Alpina, 1924

There was already an experienced and well-known mountain guide in the Inderbinen family, Ulrich's uncle Moritz, his father's brother. Ten years older than Hieronymus, Moritz already had an unusual life behind him. In the 1870s, while little more than a boy, he had left Zermatt with three or four contemporaries to seek his fortune in Canada, but the group soon scattered and he returned penniless after a few months. He then had the good fortune to encounter Dr Montagu Butler, a distinguished headmaster of Harrow and subsequently Master of Trinity College, Cambridge, an enthusiastic traveller and mountain walker who particularly loved Switzerland. The Englishman brought his ailing wife to Zermatt in 1880, three years before she died.[22]

The story was told in Moritz' obituary notice in the *Alpine Journal* written by an English mountaineer, who used to hire Ulrich's uncle as a guide for many years: "Moritz had just enough money to get home, and, after a very narrow escape from being shanghaied and robbed in New York, arrived at Visp one morning with only a few centimes in his pocket and walked home to breakfast. Not long afterwards Dr Montagu Butler was at Zermatt, and employed Moritz to help in carrying his invalid wife on short excursions in a chaise à porteur.

"Moritz was an engaging youth and could speak a little English, and Dr Butler invited him to come to England and take the position of 'general utility man'... Here Moritz spent several years [about 16]... He of course spent his summer holidays at home, and must have learned his business as a guide during this period... Moritz, who in the meantime had married an Englishwoman [Louisa Jane Pallot], returned to Zermatt, where for about ten years he pursued the calling of a guide on ordinary lines, while his wife acted as English letter-writer and English teacher for half the guides in the valley. In 1905 I had the good fortune to join Mr Freshfield on a visit to Ruwenzori, and acquired the taste for distant travel. Moritz was with me then, and also subsequently in the Himalaya (1907) and the Canadian Rockies (1909–10–11, 1913). He was immensely popular in Canada, both at the Club camps of the A.C.C. and with the packers when we were travelling in the mountains 'on our own'... 'Good old Moritz'. So his friends thought of him. I have known very few people so lovable, not one of such angelic temper."[23]

The visiting card of my uncle Moritz Inderbinen

Ulrich's uncle received his Guide's Book (*Führerbuch,* the official log and reference book for guides) in 1886, when Zermatt was entered as a resort with only three hotels. A few years after marrying in 1891 he returned home with his wife and built the Haus Vispa together with his brother Hieronymus. The locals jokingly called the area around it the

"English quarter" because of Moritz' English wife. His services as a guide were frequently sought by British guests, and he often accompanied his regular clients abroad. Photos of these trips show a distinguished group travelling with a large white dining tent that the porters had to set up at meal times in snow and ice.

Since Moritz Inderbinen and Theodul Biner, Ulrich's godfather, had earned good money as guides, Ulrich and Albinus were encouraged to take up the same line of work. After finishing his military training Ulrich investigated how to became a guide. He found he would have to complete one of the training courses run by the Swiss Alpine Club every three years. To be admitted to the course, however, he would need to fulfil a number of conditions. The rules stipulated that:

" – candidates must, among other things, be between 22 and 35 years old and fit for military service,

– enjoy a good reputation,

– have made several serious and properly certified climbs as porters in the two years preceding the course."

Ulrich was fit for military service, enjoyed a good reputation and would soon be 22, so he had no trouble with the first three conditions. Only the requirement to have made "serious and properly certified climbs" posed a problem. Never in his whole life had Ulrich climbed a mountain. As a child he had scrambled to gather edelweiss and he had walked for hours to drive the sheep but he had never stood on a "proper" mountain.

"The Matterhorn is the mountain that most strongly arouses that indefinable urge." Emil Yung, 1896

In September 1921 he decided to put an end to this situation by undertaking his first climb. The most suitable peak to start on, he decided, was his own local Matterhorn, which he knew well from below. His sister Martha, two years younger and also with a complete lack of mountaineering experience, declared herself ready to go with him. They were joined by Ulrich's friend Alfred Aufdenblatten, who had spent the summer with

Lieu du départ et désignation du voyage	Altitude Höhe	Distance Entfernung	Ausgangsstation und Bezeichnung der Reise
	met.	h. St.	
Saas, par Graechen et Hannig.		8	Saas, über Grächen und den Hannig.
— par le glacier de Balfrin.		9	— über den Balfringletscher.
— par le glacier de Ried		11	— über den Riedgletscher.
Gruben, par le Jungpass		7	Gruben, über den Jungpaß.
— par l'Augstbordpass	2900	7	— über den Augstbordpaß.
Station de Randa (1 hôtel).			**Station Randa** (1 Hotel).
Dom	4554	12	Dom.
Weisshorn	4512	18	Weißhorn.
Tæschhorn	4498	14	Taeschhorn.
Nadelgrat	4334	12	Nadelgrat.
Mettelhorn	3410	5	Mettelhorn.
Station de Zermatt (3 hôtels).			**Station Zermatt** (3 Hotels).
Mont Rose	4638	10	Monte Rosa.
Sattel du Mont Rose .	4354	7	Monte Rosa-Sattel.
Nordend	4612	12	Nordend.
Zumsteinspitze . .	4573	12	Zumsteinspitze.
Signalkuppe . . .	4561	12	Signalkuppe.
Parrotspitze . . .	4443	12	Parrotspitze.
Ludwigshöhe . .	4344	11	Ludwigshöhe.
Vincentspitze . . .	4211	12	Vincentspitze.
Jægerhorn	3975	9	Jägerhorn.
Dom	4554	14	Dom.

Lieu du départ et désignation du voyage	Altitude
Weisshorn	4…
Tæschhorn	4…
Mont Cervin.	4…
Cabane . *20*	3…
Lyskamm	4…
— et retour par le Félikjoch.	
— et descente sur Gressonay.	
Dent blanche . . .	4…
Nadelgrat , . . .	4…
Castor	4…
Pollux	4…
Rothhorn	4…
Alphubel	4…
Rimpfischhorn *46* .	4…
Strahlhorn	4…
Dent d'Hérens . .	4…
Breithorn . *35* . .	4…
— et descente sur Breuil	
Gabelhorn	4…
Untergabelhorn . .	
Allalin	4…
Petit Cervin . . .	3…
Cima de' Jazzi . .	3…
Tête blanche . . .	3…
Trifthorn	
Schallhorn	
Ebyhorn	
Theodulhorn . . .	3…
Ober-Rothhorn . .	3…
Unter-Rothhorn . .	3…

Extract from the Guide's Book from Moritz Inderbinen

108

Ausgangsstation und Bezeichnung der Reise
Weißhorn.
Täschhorn.
Matterhorn.
Schutzhütte.
Lyskamm.
— und zurück über das Felikjoch.
— und Abstieg über Gressonay.
Steinbockhorn.
Nadelgrat.
Castor.
Pollux.
Rothhorn.
Alphubel.
Rimpfischhorn.
Strahlhorn.
Dent d'Hérens.
Breithorn.
— und Abstieg über Breuil.
Gabelhorn.
Untergabelhorn.
Allalin.
Kleines Matterhorn.
Cima de' Jazzi.
Tête blanche.
Trifthorn.
Schallhorn.
Ebihorn.
Theodulhorn.
Ober-Rothhorn.
Unter-Rothhorn.

Lieu du départ et désignation du voyage	Altitude Höhe (met.)	Distance Entfernung (h. St.)	Ausgangsstation und Bezeichnung der Reise
Mettelhorn *15* . . .	3410	5	Mettelhorn.
Riffelhorn	2931	4	Riffelhorn.
Hohthæligrat . . .	3289	6	Hohthäligrat.
Gornergrat	3136	4	Gornergrat.
Riffel	2569	2	Riffel.
Hörnli	2893	4	Hörnli.
Col de Théodule . .	3333	5	Theodulpaß.
Stockje (cabane) . .		5	Stockje (Schutzhütte).
Saas, par le Domjoch .		15	Saas, über das Domjoch.
— par le Mischabeljoch	3502	14	— über das Mischabeljoch.
— par l'Alphubeljoch .	3802	12	— über das Alphubeljoch.
— par l'Allalinpass .	3570	12	— über den Allalinpaß.
— par l'Adlerpas . .	3798	12	— über den Adlerpaß.
— par l'Adlerpass avec ascension du Strahlhorn.	4191	13	— über den Adlerpaß mit Besteigung des Strahlhorn.
— par le Weissthor .	3612	12	— über das Weißthor.
Mattmark, par le glacier de Findelen et le Weissthor.		12	Mattmark, über den Findelengletscher und das Weißthor.
— par le glacier de Gorner et le Weissthor.		10	— über den Gornergletscher und das Weißthor.
— par le Schwarzgletscher .		12	— über den Schwarzgletscher.
Macugnaga, par le Weissthor.		12	Macugnaga, über das Weißthor.
— par la Cima di Roffel		12	— über die Cima di Roffel.
— par l'ancien Weissthor.	3576	14	— über das alte Weißthor.
— par le Jägerjoch .		13	— über das Jägerjoch.
Alagna, par l'Essierjoch		12	Alagna, über das Essierjoch.

his family in the neighbouring hamlet of Zum See. Alfred, too, knew the Matterhorn only from a distance, but as a porter he had several times made the relatively easy ascent of the Breithorn, one of the many "four-thousanders" around Zermatt. Alfred then persuaded one of his sisters to join them, although she too had absolutely no climbing experience.

In order not to lose time the adventure was immediately set for two days hence, 19 September. The group made their preparations quickly. They borrowed ropes and lanterns and packed food and drink. Hieronymus gave them advice from his experience of having twice reached the Rothorn hut as a porter and twice climbed the Monte Rosa.

Next day, enjoying the fine autumn weather, the four young people made their way to the Hörnli hut, which the Swiss Alpine Club had built at the foot of the Matterhorn. The girls wore skirts that reached to the ground and the nailed boots they had on every day. Ulrich and Alfred wore shirts, woollen jackets and, for this special occasion, their fine army boots, which for that time were excellent for climbing.

After a few hours they reached the Hörnli hut at 3,260 metres. As it was late in the season there were no more tourists there, and the neighbouring Hotel Belvédère (built in 1911) was already closed, so Ulrich's group was alone. The hut had been renovated only five years earlier and was in good condition, but at that time it provided no food. The ground floor had a small kitchen and dining room. Under the roof was a dormitory with 17 mattresses.

The young people drank some milk, ate pieces of rye bread with cheese and tried in vain to snatch a few hours of sleep. At 2 a.m. they eventually rose. Before leaving the hut they crossed themselves with holy water from a small stoop by the door. Outside they roped themselves together in pairs. Ulrich led his sister Martha, Alfred his sister Josephine. Then the two men grasped the lanterns, lit by flickering candles, and started looking for the way to the summit. That day there were no other climbers to lead them, so the guideless four searched by the weak light of the candles for scratches left on the rocks by the nailed boots of their predecessors. Thanks to the fine weather there was no snow or ice, so the marks were easy to find. But progress was difficult with rope in one hand and lantern in the other. Frequently the two pairs would find themselves suddenly standing in darkness after a gust of wind had blown out their candles, which they then struggled to re-light. As dawn broke, the lanterns were finally left behind and the party climbed briskly onwards.

Eventually they found themselves standing ecstatically on the summit without having wasted a single thought on the dangers they had faced. How they managed it, Ulrich does not know to this day. The descent also went smoothly. By evening he and his sister were sitting safe and sound with the family in Blatten. On a piece of paper Martha testified to the climb, bringing her brother a step closer to being admitted to the guides' training course. But Ulrich has never understood how his parents agreed to such a dangerous undertaking.

"Few villagers can find work elsewhere or have enough livestock and well-stocked storehouses to survive the winter without worry." J. Jegerlehner, 1923

In October 1921 Ulrich again looked in vain for work elsewhere as Zermatt still offered no means of earning money in the winter. The railway from Visp, even 30 years after its opening, ran only in the summer, so every winter the village sank into its long sleep. In his book *The Lost Valley,* Hannes Taugwalder (born 1910) described the Zermatt winters of the 1920s: "In the first half of September the last holiday-makers left the Matterhorn village. They were followed by a stampede of shopkeepers. As the grocers on the main street came without exception from outside the village, almost all the shops shut. ... The hotel fronts were closed, the shutters bolted, the verandas boarded up, doorways and service entrances blocked, ... Old Zermatt life prevailed once more in the village street: the slow tread of nailed shoes, the baskets and milk churns on bent backs. Cattle, goats and sheep jangled along the main street. The inhabitants were at home with each other again."

As usual, Ulrich helped his parents with the daily work in winter. He used his free time to learn English with some of the other men who wanted to become guides. The teacher was his aunt Louisa Jane, wife of Moritz. She received her willing pupils in the parlour of her apartment on the second floor of the Haus Vispa.

Die alte Hörnlihütte in der wir 1921 übernachteten

The old Hörnli Hut in which we spent the night in 1921.

As spring came Ulrich found work on the Gornergrat railway. Every year in May the snow had to be shovelled away from the tracks before the railway could open. Sixty men were needed for two or three weeks to clear more than six miles of line. In the early morning the train would take the workers to the point at which they had stopped the day before. In this way Ulrich enjoyed his first trip on the mountain railway. He slaved every day for ten hours for a daily wage of seven francs. The work was especially arduous where avalanches had come down across the line. In some places the snowdrifts were twelve metres high.

In the brief midday breaks the men sat outside on the rails eating polenta cooked in a large black pot over an open fire. When Ulrich returned home tired at the end of the day he stuffed his wet boots with newspaper and set them by the kitchen stove, but invariably they were still damp in the morning when he had to put them on again.

In the winter of 1922 Ulrich was the only Zermatter to find work building a dam in Mauvoisin. Even more than in St Maurice and Amsteg he felt himself alone and abandoned. The young men with whom he shared the workers' huts branded him an outsider and shut him out of their group. His unpleasant experiences that winter reinforced his determination to become a guide. He hoped thereby to earn enough money to become independent of work outside his home village.

In Zermatt in March 1923 Peter Taugwalder died at the age of 80. He had been one of the seven men who made the first ascent of the Matterhorn in 1865. He, with his father and Edward Whymper, survived the accident that killed Michel Croz, a famous guide from Chamonix, and the Englishmen Lord Francis Douglas, the Rev. Charles Hudson (vicar of Skillington, Lincolnshire) and Douglas Hadow. The circumstances of the accident had given rise to much speculation. As the 19-year-old Hadow slipped during the descent, endangering the whole group, the rope broke between Lord Douglas and Peter Taugwalder's father, allowing Douglas and his three colleagues fall to their deaths. For a long time the older Taugwalder was suspected of having cut the rope in order to save himself and his son. His wounded hands, the torn rope showing no sign of cuts, and even exoneration by a judicial inquiry were not enough to dispel suspicion altogether.

Ulrich had heard the story already as a child and had frequently seen Peter Taugwalder sitting on a bench in the church square but he had never dared to speak to the withdrawn old man. He was convinced that the man's father was innocent. How could he have cut the rope so quickly with a rickety knife without being observed by Whymper, who stood behind him?

Whymper himself defended Taugwalder against the accusation but denigrated him in other ways, making himself deeply unpopular in the valley. But the Zermatters never uttered a word of complaint to the Alpine Club. Eventually Sir Arnold Lunn, the British writer, came to the defence of the Taugwalders and gave his opinion of Whymper: "...a pathetic and friendless man... Few men climbed with Whymper for more than one season. His guides, with the exception perhaps of Croz and Almer, disliked him... He was not lovable nor, apart from mountaineering, an admirable man, but it is impossible to deny him the unmistakeable imprint of greatness."[24]

Summer 1923, on the way to the Breithorn

In the summer of 1923 Ulrich went up the mountains as a porter to collect another certificate to qualify for the guides' course. With the guide Simon Julen he accompanied a female guest up the 4,164-metre

Die Gandegghütte

The Gandegg Hut

Breithorn, carrying the lady's rucksack for a fee of 30 francs a day. A photo of this two-day tour shows him wearing a shirt, tie and jacket next to the stout lady, who, he recalls, "had enough of herself to carry". On the first day the three took the Gornergrat Railway as far as Rotenboden, the penultimate station at an altitude of 2,815 metres. From there they continued on foot over the Gorner Glacier to the Gandegg Hut, where they spent the night. Next morning they started the ascent of the Breithorn, reaching the summit in four hours. The descent to Zermatt was achieved the same day and Ulrich had the climb certified on a piece of paper.

Next summer he was called up for military service. He attended the infantry school for non-commissioned officers in Berne and was promoted to corporal, then a year later to sergeant.

> *"The mountain guide is the medium through which the spirit of a place speaks to us."*   F. O. Wolf, 1886

In the spring of 1925 Ulrich and Albinus applied for the guides' course in Siders from 15–25 July. Ulrich sent in his application with the two slips of paper certifying his ascents of the Matterhorn and the Breithorn. He thereby fulfilled all the conditions for attending the course. Altogether 55 candidates were accepted, of whom 20 came from Zermatt.

Half of the ten days of the course were dedicated to theoretical study. For the practical part there was a four-day climbing expedition. Ulrich's group went to the Mountet Hut and from there made several practice climbs. Different techniques, such as climbing on ice and rock, were taught. On the last day, after passing his exam, Ulrich and 45 other candidates received their Guides' Books, diplomas and badges.

On the first pages of the Guide's Book the duties of a guide were described by the "Decree of 13 February 1925 concerning Mountain Guides" and by the "Instructions for mountain guides". Ulrich had already studied these texts in the theoretical part of his course. They read in part as follows: "Guides are obliged to render services to travellers who request them. They will attend their clients with the utmost discretion and courtesy and obey their orders in so far as these can be reconciled with the safety of the expedition."

Monte Rosa section of the Swiss Alpine Club. Timetable for mountain guides' course in Siders, 15–25 June 1925. Monday: Organization; geography of Switzerland; map reading; insurance; emergency signals; map reading. Tuesday: Care of the injured, geography of Valais; using huts; rescue work; equipment for guides and tourists; use of the compass. Wednesday: Geography of Valais; regulations for guides; care of the injured; practice on rocks combined with emergency signals and transport of the injured. Thursday: Practice tour (practical instruction). Friday: Geography of Switzerland; map reading; care of the injured; regulations for guides; dangers in the high mountains; geography of Valais. Saturday: Map reading; duties of the guide towards travellers and expeditions; dangers in the high mountains; hygiene and cleanliness; the Swiss Alpine Club and other alpine clubs. Sunday-Wednesday: Extended tour, special programme. Thursday: Exams and discharge. Siders, 15 May 1925. Director C. Dübelbeiss

Sektion Monte-Rosa des S.A.C.

Stundenplan des Führerkurses vom 15.-25. Juni 1925 in Siders.

Tag	7½-9.00 (8.00-9.00)	9.00-10½	10½-12.00	2-3.00	3-4.00	4-6.00
Montag 15.VI.25	Organisation	Geographie der Schweiz	Kartenlesen	Versicherung	Notsignale	Kartenlesen
Dienstag 16.VI.	Samariter-dienst	Geographie des Kt. Wallis	Hütten-reglement	Rettungs-stationen & Rettungswesen	Ausrüstung von Führer und Touristen	Gebrauch der Bussole
Mittwoch 17.VI.	Geographie des Kt. Wallis	Führer-reglement	Samariter-dienst	Uebung im Felsen, in Verbindung mit Notsignalen, Transport Verunglükter.		
Donnerstag 18.VI.	Uebungstour (Prakt. Unterricht.)					
Freitag 19.VI.	Geographie der Schweiz	Kartenlesen	Samariter-dienst	Führer-reglement	Gefahren des Hochgebirges	Geographie des Wallis
Samstag 20.VI.	Kartenlesen	Pflichten der Führer geg. Reisenden & u. Karawanen	Gefahren des Hochgebirges	Hygiene & Reinlichkeit	Der S.A.C. und andere alpine Vereine	
Sonntag 21.VI. bis **Mittwoch** 24.VI.	Grosse Bergtour nach Spezialprogramm.					
Donnerstag 25.VI.	Examen & Entlassung					

Siders, 15. Mai 1925.

Der Leiter: C. Dübelbeiss

Even the desirable characteristics of guides were listed in detail. In first place stood courtesy:

"The guide will always be aware that he is in the service of the traveller and is paid by him; he will therefore not alienate the traveller by being rude, pestering him or giving him false information."

In second place came technical skill, physical strength and a realistic assessment of the capabilities of the traveller:

For the practical part of the guiding course we went to the Mountet Hut.

120

wir in die Mountet Hütte

"The novice climber will need the supporting hand of the guide in situations where the experienced climber will reject it. The guide must endeavour not to offend the latter with unnecessary intrusiveness, any more than he may expose the former to danger by neglecting to render the necessary help."

Full of good resolutions, Ulrich and Albinus returned to Zermatt looking forward eagerly to their first season as guides. But before they could seek work they had to help their parents bring in the hay. Hieronymus and Maria could not manage it with only the help of 14-year-old Medard and 11-year-old Veronika. Their oldest daughter, Maria, had been married in the spring and was no longer available; Franziska worked in Kreuzlingen; Martha had found a position with a family in Kriens; Monika helped the keeper of the Gandegg Hut; and Berta assisted her mother with the housework.

Thus it was not until the third week in July that Ulrich and Albinus moved into the apartment in the Haus Vispa, which was unoccupied in summer. Every morning they mingled with the 100 guides who waited for clients in the Bahnhofstrasse. The competition was intense. Lacking a single reference in his book, Ulrich found it difficult to convince potential clients of his qualities. Albinus and other newly qualified guides shared his fate.

"One needs to be a mule to get regular work."

The older mountain guides had an easier time because they could draw on years of experience and had gradually built up a base of regular clients. An extra advantage was enjoyed by guides from the neighbouring villages of Täsch, Randa and St Niklaus because they could make contact with visitors on the train up the valley. Often they arrived in Zermatt with bookings already made.

Ulrich and Albinus suffered another disadvantage by coming from a farming family as new young guides were particularly dependent on recommendations from hotels or older colleagues. This was explained in a newspaper article on Zermatt: "A word about choosing a guide... Every

Das Foto aus meinem Führerbuch

The photo from my Guide's Book

porter, every chambermaid, every head waiter... has a brother or cousin or other relative who earns his living as a guide and therefore belongs to the inventory of the hotel... Unfortunately not all guides have these good connections..." (*Alpina,* December 1924).

I (on the left) and my colleagues wait for clients.

That was the position of Ulrich and Albinus. Among all their relatives none worked in the hotel trade. Nor were the other guides in the family any help. Theodul Biner, Ulrich's godfather, had died in 1923. Moritz Inderbinen, who could have given his nephew valuable support in getting started, had fallen ill. So Ulrich sat with his colleagues from dawn to dusk on the wall outside the Hotel Monte Rosa, well-dressed, with his

Guide's Book in a small leather pouch, waiting to be accosted by a visitor. He was too shy to take the initiative and volunteer his services.

The young guides watched the lively scene in the Bahnhofstrasse, and in the afternoons they listened to orchestras playing in the garden of the Hotel Zermatterhof. Elegant foreigners strolled by. Simple local women, bent under the weight of the "Tschiffra", came in from the fields. Hotel employees transported great blocks of ice that they had hacked out of the Gorner Glacier to cool drinks and food. Porters with gold braid on their uniforms watched out for guests. The lift boy at the Hotel Monte Rosa, young Hannes Taugwalder, stood in his fine uniform in front of the hotel and saw off departing guests in the hope of a small tip. Horse-drawn carriages brought in new tourists, most of them with numerous cases for a stay of several weeks. Heavily laden mules were driven past taking provisions up to the mountain huts. "One needs to be a mule to get regular work", remarked one of Ulrich's colleagues, who had also waited many days in vain for an engagement.

At the end of July it finally happened. The seemingly endless waiting paid off. A German doctor from Krefeld, who needed two guides for an ascent of the Matterhorn, engaged Ulrich and 42-year-old Alexander Perren. In the early afternoon of 28 July the two guides picked up their client at the hotel and made their way to the Hörnli Hut. Ulrich's equipment was extremely simple. He wore warm trousers, a shirt, a woollen jacket, his army boots and socks knitted by his mother. After two hours of climbing the three men took a brief pause at the chapel of "Our Lady of the Snow". Two hours later they reached the Hörnli Hut and handed their food to the hut keeper, who made it into a modest evening meal.

After a short night's sleep the two guides and their customer started out again at 2 a.m. On leaving the hut the men took holy water from the stoop near the door, crossed themselves and said a short prayer. Outside Ulrich lit the candles in the lanterns. It was dark and cold; even in summer the night temperature was often below freezing point at this altitude of over 3,000 metres.

The climb went smoothly, and Ulrich acquired the first entry in his book: "On 29.7.25 Mr Ulrich Inderbinen accompanied me up the Matterhorn with Alexander Perren. Mr Inderbinen showed himself thoroughly safe and reliable, so I hope to climb with him more frequently."

After this first successful climb there followed another week of waiting. The second entry in Ulrichs book is dated 6–7 August. With two Swiss mountaineers he undertook the traverse of the Wellenkuppe and Obergabelhorn. After another and longer interval – nine days – he received his third and last engagement for that summer, taking three Germans up the Breithorn. They also praised his professional and human qualities. Thus in his first season as a guide Ulrich brought back earnings only on three days.

"It is foolish to believe that winter health holidays and Alpine winter sports are merely a passing fad."

Walliser Bote, October 1911

In the autumn Ulrich and Albinus registered for a ski guides' course planned for December in Zermatt, but lack of snow caused it to be postponed until the beginning of March 1926, by which time the skiing conditions were good. Only qualified mountain guides were admitted and the fee was 20 francs. Participants from elsewhere stayed for 9 francs a

On 16/17 August 1925 Mr Ulrich
Inderbinen led Dr K. Bach, Dr
E. Kinkel and me up the Breithorn.
We can confirm that as a guide he
was particularly efficient and relia-
ble, and as a companion friendly.
We are in every respect very satis-
fied with him.

night, including board, at the Hotel Alpina, which was specially opened
and heated for the purpose. With 47 colleagues Ulrich received a week of
theoretical and practical instruction. At the end they had to take a test
which was set as follows:

"Exam, start 8 a.m. Candidates accompanied by HH. Experts will go to
steep slope about 15 minutes above Zermatt. Each will descend in the
stem position and then be accorded the appropriate mark."

Ulrich's mark was 1.25, so he ranked as a good skier. After also passing
a theoretical exam he received his ski guide's diploma. Like all Zermatt
guides he hoped that the railway from Visp would soon start a winter
service and bring lots of winter visitors, so ski guiding seemed to offer
good prospects. Up to then, local men had had to earn their money for
the whole year within a few weeks in summer.

In the spring of 1926 Ulrich's uncle Moritz Inderbinen died at the age
of 70. Ulrich was working at that time, as he had done for the past four

Skiführerkurs in Zermatt.~

vom 6.–12. Dezember 1925.

organisiert durch den h. Staatsrat des Kt. Wallis, und des S.A.C., Sektion Mte Rosa, (vertreten durch Hr. C. Dübelbeiss, Vizepräsident der Sektion, in Siders.)

Kursleiter: H.H.   Schaller Adolf,   Führer,   Zermatt
     "   Perren Gottfried   "   "
     "   Julen Anton   "   "
     "   Dr. N. Volken, Arzt,
     "   Julen Felix,   Präs. Skiklub,
     "   Dübelbeiss C.,   Delegierter der Sektion Mte. Rosa,   Siders.

Teilnehmer: Nur patentierte Führer werden zum Kurse zugelassen.
(s. Führerreglement 1925, Art. 19–22)

Programm.

Sonntag, den 6. Dezember 25

16°° h   Besammlung der Teilnehmer im Führerlokal. – Appel & Gruppeneinteilung.
17°° h   Besprechung des Kurses.
          Vortrag über Hygenie des Wintersportes. (Dr. Volken)

Montag, den 7. Dezember

8°° h – 12°° h   Uebungsfahren (Schwünge – Stemmbogen etc.)
14°° – 17°° h   Theorie über Skiarten, Skibehandlung, Bindungen, Reparaturen, techn. Hilfsmittel.

Dienstag, 8. Dezember.

8°° – 12°° h   Uebungsfahren – Seilfahren
14°° – 17°° h   Theorie über Lawinenbildung, der verschiedenen Schneearten, Gletscher im Winter.
20°° h   Lichtbildervortrag: Der Ski im Hochgebirge. (Jng. A. Perren)

Mittwoch, den 9. Dez.

8°° h   Kleinere Tagestour nach Karte & Kompass. – Geländeausnützung.
          Anstiegspuren, Abfahrten an steilem Hang, u.s.w.
18°° h   Vortrag & Demonstrationen über Rettungsdienst, Notverbände etc.
                                           (Dr. Volken)

Donnerstag, den 10. Dez.

8°° – 11°° h   Bau von Rettungsschlitten & Verwundeten-Transporte auf Ski.
13°° h   Aufstieg zur Betempshütte (2802 m)
19°° h   Vortrag über Hüttenordnung & Pflichten des Führers.

Freitag, den 11. Dez.

          Besteigung der Cima di Jazzi 3818 m und Rückfahrt über Findelengletscher nach Zermatt.

Samstag, den 12. Dez.

8°° – 12°°   Leistungsprüfung vor Expertenkommission
14°° – 15.30   Vortrag über das Versicherungswesen; Kenntnis der Winterhochtouren und ihrer Stützpunkte.
16.°°   Entlassung. Schluss des Kurses.

                                           Die Kursleitung

Programme:

Sunday 6 December:
Assembly of participants in Guides' Office; roll call and assignment to groups.
Discussion of course; lecture on hygiene and winter sports (Dr Volken).

Monday 7 December:
Practice run (swings, stem turns etc.).
Theory of different types of ski, ski handling, bindings, repairs, technical assistance.

Tuesday 8 December:
Practice runs, skiing while roped.
Theory of avalanches, different types of snow, glaciers in winter. Slide lecture on high Alpine skiing (engineer A. Perren).

Wednesday 9 December:
Short day tour using map and compass – exploiting the terrain, climbing tracks, descending steep slopes, etc.
Lecture and demonstration on rescue service, first aid etc. (Dr Volken).

Thursday 10 December:
Constructing rescue sledges and transporting the injured on skis.
Climb to Betemps hut (2802 metres).
Lecture on using huts, and duties of the guide.

Friday 11 December:
Ascent of the Cima di Jazzi (3818 metres) and return via Findeln glacier to Zermatt.

Saturday 12 December
Tests supervised by commission of experts.
Lecture on insurance; knowledge of winter tours and refuges.
Discharge. End of course.

years, shovelling snow from the Gornergrat railway. This led to a curious and sad episode. He was so deeply tanned from working outside in the sun that when he tried to visit his dying uncle he was barred from the room because the whole family feared that Moritz would think his nephew was the devil. With Moritz's death Ulrich and Albinus lost an important figure in their lives. They had learnt from their difficulty in finding work the previous year that above all they lacked good connections. Their uncle's death deprived them of a link to the regular clients Moritz had accumulated over the years.

Albinus started his own family in May and moved with his wife to the old priest's house in the Church Square. Martha also married and followed her husband to St Niklausen in the canton of Lucerne.

The hay and rye were gathered late that summer because of bad weather. At the beginning of July 40 centimetres of new snow fell in Zermatt, so Ulrich could not start guiding until mid-August. Two weeks later the season was over. Nevertheless, from 14–29 August he worked almost every day. All the entries in his book emphasise not only his excellent skills as a climber but also his good care of his clients and his modesty. For the first time he was engaged for several days by a guest from Stettin. Even so, his second season was disappointing. After such a short summer he had earned only 550 francs, far less than he had expected.

In the winter Ulrich had to take on an increasing number of duties for which his father was becoming too old. Medard, who had finished school in the spring, helped him. The brothers cared for the sheep, fetched wood and litter from Zmutt and Blatten, split logs for burning and repaired the cowsheds, barns and storehouses. There was no lack of work.

The summer of 1927 brought Zermatt a modest boom. The railway from Visp carried 96,000 travellers, the Gornergrat Railway nearly 52,000, thus restoring traffic at last to its pre-war level.

After the harvest had been gathered, Ulrich embarked on his third season as a mountain guide. In spite of his good references the summer was no better than the previous one. A single climb in July was followed by few engagements in August. Ulrich's weekly earnings lay between 50 and 200 francs, varying according to the difficulty of the ascents. The fee for the Breithorn was 50 francs, for the Matterhorn 130 francs. These fees included walking up to a hut the day before the climb. For longer engagements Ulrich received 30 francs per day regardless of how many, or which, ascents he undertook. When the weather was bad, this arrangement benefited the guide because fewer climbs were ventured, while in good weather it worked to the advantage of the guest.

Although the fees seem high for those days, they were not so good when taking into account the short summer season and the long waiting times. Like his colleagues in this period, Ulrich spent an average of four days each week waiting for clients.

From time to time he could earn money from rescue work. The regulations stipulated that all licensed guides were obliged "in case of acci-

The telescope in front of the Hotel Mont Cervin.
We unemployed guides observe our colleagues on the Matterhorn.

dents to take part in search and rescue operations". For this they were paid. Most accidents took place on the Matterhorn, which attracted more and more climbers. Since the first ascent by Whymper in 1865 the mountain had already claimed 50 lives.

When climbers were reported missing the rescue teams set out at night so as to begin searching at dawn. After the rescue the injured or dead mountaineers were carried from the scene of the accident to the Schwarzsee. When the terrain permitted they were carried on stretchers but on steep slopes they had to be taken in body bags. At the Schwarzsee a mule would be waiting with a sledge for the rest of the journey. The rescue sledges – unlike the transport sledges used in winter – had wooden skids without metal runners. They were dragged down to Zermatt over the meadows and rough tracks by mules and several men.

The year 1928 was a good one for Ulrich. While harvesting in summer he met his future wife, Anna Aufdenblatten, who was gathering hay with her mother. Born in 1897, Anna had lost her father at the age of three. He was killed in an accident while working in the forest. As the oldest of four children she had to take on the duties of an adult at an early age and look after her three younger siblings. After finishing school she worked for two years as a household servant in Paris. Returning with a good knowledge of French, she immediately found a job in the Hotel Zermatterhof. In her free time she helped her mother with the housework and in the fields.

Anna and Ulrich did not think of marriage at first. Hieronymus could not support another family on what he earned from farming, and Ulrich's modest income was insufficient to sustain a family of his own. His low earnings as guide could be supplemented in spring by 200–300 francs for shovelling snow on the Gornergrat railway, but he received nothing for helping his father, so his total annual income was scarcely more than 1,000 francs.

In the summer of 1928 there was a deterioration in working conditions for guides. The local authority stopped them touting for business at the station, thereby sharpening competition outside the hotels. Guides who had sought clients at the station, or even from the steps of the trains, shifted their activities to the hotels. Ulrich had no way of attracting attention to himself.

Mit meinen Kollegen berge ich einen
verletzten Bergsteiger

With my colleagues I rescue an injured climber.

Die Kapelle "Maria zum Schnee" am

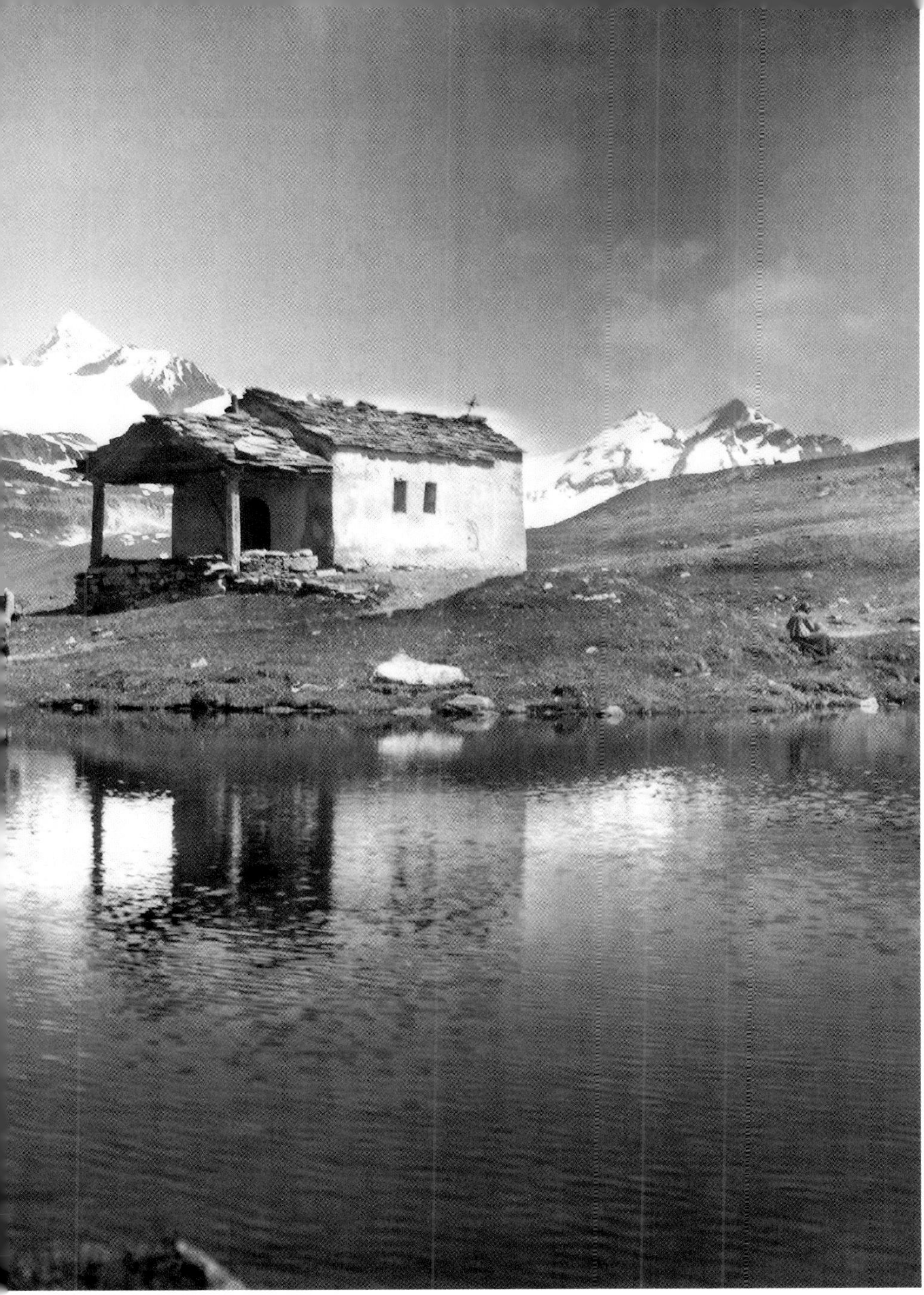

Schwarzsee

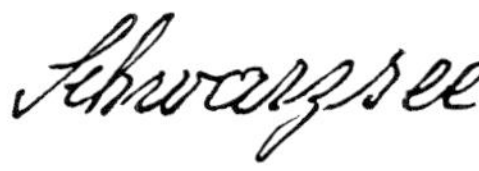

The chapel of "Our Lady of the Snow" at Schwarzsee

"...the mountains are a magical world, the Gornergrat supremely overwhelming because its views extend into fantastic and gigantic realms." François Gos, 1925

Eventually, Ulrich and Albinus found a way of avoiding the stiff competition in the village. They rose early every morning and walked up to the top station of the Gornergrat Railway, where they waited for the arrival of the first tourists. By making the four-hour climb to 3,100 metres on foot they saved the train fare. Visitors emerging from the trains would survey the imposing panorama of "four-thousanders" and be inspired to book a climb. Then they would spot the two men, the only guides there, conveniently positioned with their round guides' badges. Clients were also directed to them by the man responsible for the telescope at the summit.

One day a woman came up to Ulrich wanting to undertake a two-day tour to the Hörnli Hut – normally a simple mountain walk that takes a few hours. Ulrich accepted the somewhat unusual request with joy. The overnight stay at the Hörnli Hut would be very welcome because he would be paid for two days and would therefore earn 60 francs.

Next morning he fetched the lady from her hotel and the two of them took the train to Rotenboden. From there they crossed the Gorner Glacier and reached their destination in the afternoon. Ulrich spent the night in the dormitory of the hut with the other guides while his guest took a room next door in the better equipped Hotel Belvédère, which could accommodate 40 people.

Eating together at the hotel, Ulrich and his guest fell into conversation with two men who wanted to climb the Matterhorn next morning but were still looking for a guide. Ulrich was lucky. The lady who had booked him for two days encouraged him to take on the job. She offered to wait for him at the Belvédère until the following day.

At 2 a.m. next morning Ulrich set off to climb the Matterhorn with the two men, returning to the hut in the early afternoon. There he rejoined the lady from the previous day and led her back to Zermatt via Schwarzsee and Stafelalp. On the way down they met many tourists riding up to Schwarzsee on horses or mules, the women among them on side-saddles accompanied by mule drivers.

The Gornergrat Railway

On arriving back in the village Ulrich took his guest to her hotel and thanked her for her generosity, which had brought him double earnings. Then he immediately walked four hours back up to the Hotel Belvédère, where the two men with whom he had climbed the Matterhorn were waiting with their wives. They had engaged him to take them up the Breithorn next day.

By the end of the summer of 1928 Ulrich had eight entries in his Guide's Book by Swiss and foreign mountaineers. Since most of the engagements were for several days he had been comparatively busy from

13th August 1928, Ulrich
Inderbinen was my personal
guide in the traverse of the
Untergabelhorn, climbing all
the "Gendarms". The next day
he guided me in the traverse of
the Wellenkup and the Obergable-
horn. In every kind of climbing
which we experienced: snow, rock,
glissades, and glacier, he proved
himself skilful. Especially, helpful
to the beginner, telling him where
to put hands and feet, he is always
ready and alert to save one from
slipping or falling and quick to
get one out of difficulty.
    I am happy to recommend
him to anyone, especially one who
has never done any rock-climbing
before, as a skilful, helpful
guide in any kind of climbing.

            Jonathan B. Bingham
Zermatt, 15th August, 1928.
            Mitchell Bingham
    Brewster Bingham

This tour was mentioned in the *Journal de Zermatt,* to which in those days climbs were reported. "Tourists are earnestly entreated to inform the editors of the *Fremdenliste* of climbs they have undertaken."

Chronique des Ascensions.

Le 12 août, le Riffelhorn, le 13 Untergabelhorn par les gendarmes, le 14 la traversée de l'Obergabelhorn ont été faits par les 3 frères Bingham avec les guides Alexandre Perren, Gottfried Perren et Inderbinnen Ulrich.

Le 18 août, Mr John B. Aspegren a fait, partant de la cabane de Schönbühl, l'ascension du Cervin par l'arête de Z'mutt et descente sur le Hörnli avec le guide Sigismond Perren.

Deux alpinistes neuchâtelois, M. Leuba, fils du médecin de Fleurier, et M. Reymond, de Neuchâtel, qui avaient fait Mercredi l'ascension du Besso, ont disparu. Déjà mercredi soir, u e colonne de secours, partie de Zinal, est allée à leur recherche, un orage ayant éclaté sur la région. La colonne a retrouvé les sacs au pied de la dernière montée, mais pas trace des alpinistes.
Jeudi et vendredi, la colonne a repris ses recherches mais sans résultats.

Extract from *Journal de Zermatt*, 1928

On the Gornergrat

the middle of July to the end of August. He also led his first regular client, an Englishman named Sergei de Vesselitsky, with whom he had done several climbs the previous summer and who remained faithful to him for many more years. Mr de Vesselitsky (1882–1957) was an ardent and popular member of the Alpine Club who normally spent August at the Monte Rosa hotel. Nicknamed "Old Vladivostok" because of his Russian origin, he had been London correspondent of Novoe Vremya until the Russian revolution. In 1931 he changed his name to Merriman when he inherited some property.[25]

In the autumn Ulrich was able to work for several weeks for the municipality, helping to build a new bridge over the stream above

140

This summer Ulrich Inderbinen accompanied me as guide on two expeditions, both undertaken while I was still convalescing from an illness. On July 21st 1928 he took me up the Rimpfischhorn, while on July 26th he guided me very skilfully up the Obergabelhorn (via the Wellenkuppe), returning by the Arbengrat and Arbengletscher. I take pleasure in confirming my previous estimate of his proficiency. He combines great energy and keenness with prudence and painstaking attention to details.

S. de Vesselitsky, Ph.D, F.R.G.S.
A.C. and S.A.C.
Zermatt July 28th, 1928.

Zmutt. The old wooden bridge, which had been used for decades by the inhabitants of the hamlet, had long threatened to collapse. Only one person and one animal were allowed on it at any one time.

The workers constructed the new bridge on the left side of the gulley, then stretched two ropes across and pushed the whole bridge along the ropes until one end reached the other side. For their work they were paid five francs a day.

At the end of the year a new epoch opened for Zermatt. The railway from Visp began its long-awaited winter service with one train a day from 21 December to the end of February. Thus ended a long tale of woe. As early as 1904 the service had been called for in order to "promote some of the villages in the valley, principally Zermatt, to winter resorts... The people who work in the tourist industry in the summer would then find work in the winter too, and would be less exposed to the undeniable dangers of idleness in the long slack period," according to the *Walliser Bote.*

In November 1911 an "initiative committee" had published a two-page petition to the State Council "concerning the winter service of the Visp–

The old bridge over the Zmutt stream

Zermatt Railway". Even at that stage the committee had described its request as a matter of life or death for the tourist industry: "The people of the Visp valley have an ever more urgent need to earn money in winter because of rising prices, but they also require the train for moral reasons".

When, at long last, the conditions for a winter service had been agreed, the outbreak of the First World War destroyed all hopes of an early start. Thus it was not until 1926 – twenty-two years after the first demand – that the project was taken up again. The following year the winter trains ran as far as St Niklaus. A year later they finally reached Zermatt. The Gornergrat Railway also started its first winter season, running two trains a day as far as Riffelalp between Christmas and February. At that time five hotels were open, accommodating 942 guests.

Next summer the hay could be brought in early, so Ulrich started work as a guide from the middle of July. His clients came, as in the previous year, from England, Germany and Switzerland.

When he had finished his summer season and done his army refresher course he spent the late autumn in Zmutt. His family had become smaller since the marriages of Maria, Martha and Albinus. The six children who still lived with their parents had grown up, while the youngest daughter, Veronika, was in her last year of school. Maria and Hieronymus received a lot of help from their children and found at last a little time for leisure.

One evening in November Ulrich had an experience he never forgot. With his parents, brothers and sisters he was sitting comfortably in the little parlour of their house in Zmutt when an inexplicable noise came suddenly from the empty kitchen. Then there was deathly quiet. No one dared go to see what had happened. Hieronymus cast a stricken look at his family and said sadly: "Next year we shall no longer all be together."

In the second touristic winter season the railway from Visp ran from the middle of December to the end of February with two trains a day. The hotels in Zermatt were fully booked, providing about 1,000 guest beds. Winter visitors thus outnumbered the inhabitants, of whom there were now 962. Theodor Wundt, who visited the village in the winter of 1929–30, wrote:

"Now there is a lively winter life in the resort. The shops are open and in the streets, just as in summer, the guides walk to and fro with pipes in

In the summer of 1929 on the Leiterspitze

Ulrich Inderbinen has acted as guide for me and some friends for a month. We have done the Breithorn Castor Obergabelhorn Dufourspitze Nordend Wellenkuppe ∧ Zmutt arete of Matterhorn Dent Blanche - Zinal Rothorn - and Rimpfischhorn -

On all occasions his guiding has been sure reliable & such as to inspire confidence. A quality in him which is very satisfactory is that he is ready to go on in the face of poor conditions both of weather & mountain though the responsibility of such devolves upon him. In this way we have got some of the peaks that we might not otherwise have done. I can recommend him with great confidence. M. Bevanthorn A.C.

Zermatt Aug 10./1930

their mouths. ... The hotels provide not only comfort but also a varied and entertaining social life with concerts, dances, carnivals, excursions, picnics and competitions."

Like many other guides, Ulrich sought work as a ski guide but the time for guided ski tours had not yet come. He did not find a single client.

On 4 March 1930 Hieronymus's prophecy came true with the death of Ulrich's mother from pneumonia at the age of 61. Ulrich and Anna had to postpone their marriage, which had been planned for May, in order to observe the obligatory year of mourning.

In the summer the railway, which had been electrified the previous year, extended its line from Visp to Brig. From then on it called itself the Brig–Visp–Zermatt-Bahn (BVZ). Ulrich, now in his fifth season as guide, had two long-term engagements. A group of British mountaineers engaged him for a month.

After that he spent a whole week with his faithful client Mr de Vesselitsky. One day as he was climbing with him on the Signalkuppe the weather suddenly closed in. Only with a struggle did the two men reach the Capanna Margherita hut. There they sat through the whole of Saturday afternoon as it was impossible to go on. Not until next morning did the snowstorm let up a little, allowing Ulrich to risk the descent to the village. He knew what awaited him: a furious father who had no understanding for the very good reason why his son had missed Mass on Sunday.

"My first tour as a ski guide"

Next winter snow was plentiful. Avalanches repeatedly brought train services to a standstill, creating a welcome source of income for local men, who shovelled the track free for modest pay.

In January Ulrich was able to earn his first 50 francs as a ski guide. A young Swedish visitor engaged him to climb the Breithorn. On the evening before the ascent Ulrich prepared both pairs of skis. At that time he possessed no climbing skins so he made do with thin rope which he cleverly wound around the skis.

At 4 a.m. on a bitterly cold morning the two men set out from Zermatt. Ulrich was poorly equipped. He wore his normal wool jacket with a warm pullover underneath, and he was still using his old, far too long skis with primitive bindings and no steel edges.

The route took them via Hermetje, Schwarzsee and the Theodul Glacier. After ten hours of climbing they reached the summit of the Breithorn. There they removed the ropes from the skis and started on what should have been the more enjoyable part of the day, the descent to Zer-

8.1.1931
A splendid if very cold ski expedition to Zermatt's Breithorn. I thank the energetic guide for a good tour. Bad snow, bad conditions. Unfortunately, shortly before our descent of the glacier my guide injured his right foot. In spite of that, a good run home. Altogether 14 hours. Thanks to my guide, all went well in spite of the weather.

matt. But the exhilaration of the descent was soon spoiled. On an icy patch at the bottom of the glacier Ulrich's skis lost their grip. He fell, and had to struggle on in great pain to Schwarzsee. There the pain in his right leg was so unbearable that he took off his skis, bound them together, sat on them and slid slowly downhill accompanied by his client. After two hours they reached Zum See. There Ulrich deposited his skis in his father's sheepshed and, supporting himself on his ski sticks, hobbled via Blatten down to Zermatt, where he immediately went to the doctor. But when Dr Volken heard that Ulrich had made his own way down from the glacier to the village in four hours he ruled out the possibility of a broken leg and sent his patient home with ointment for sprains.

Blatten in the snow

Nevertheless Ulrich's pain got steadily worse. Next day he took the train to the doctor in St Niklaus, who had an X-ray machine. The picture showed clearly a broken fibula. The leg was put in plaster, and Ulrich had to walk with crutches for several weeks. For the first time in his life he was condemned to inactivity.

That spring the BVZ Railway company began to build numerous tunnels and galleries to protect the track against avalanches. Ulrich, who by this time had recovered from his accident, used the chance to earn money by working in the off-season on avalanche barriers between Täsch and Zermatt. He saved his wages for his future family. As the year of mourning for his mother had now passed, his wedding with Anna was due to take place soon. But he had to change his plans once again. Shortly before the wedding Anna's mother fell so ill that she needed her eldest daughter to look after her.

In 1931 the railway carried 227,000 passengers. In spite of this record number the crisis in the world economy was slowly making itself felt. Only about a quarter of the tourists took the train up to Gornergrat. Many saved on hiring guides by not undertaking guided excursions. Ulrich did not get his first client until 20 July and finished his season as early as 15 August.

In the autumn Anna's mother died, so another year of mourning meant that the wedding had to be postponed yet again, this time to the spring after next.

In the summer of 1932 the world recession began to make a serious impact. The recovery that had begun after the end of the war faltered. The BVZ carried only half the numbers of the passengers of the previous year.

Ulrich's work as a guide began with a 14-day engagement by a New Zealander. He remembers that while climbing the Matterhorn the man's purse fell out of his pocket and notes worth more than 700 francs swirled in the air and floated slowly down the mountain to disappear for ever. But Ulrich was still paid for his services.

For the first time the season extended beyond August. Ulrich's last tour was on 7 September. In the winter, however, he could still find no work as a ski guide, so the only employment open to him was helping his father on the land and with the animals.

In the summer of 1933 on the Riffelhorn

After the wedding had been postponed three times Ulrich and Anna were finally married in May 1933 in the church of St Mauritius. The official marriage had taken place the previous day. As was the custom in those days, the bride wore black and the wedding was at 6 o'clock on a Saturday morning so that work would not be affected. Among those present were Hieronymus and the brothers and sisters of Ulrich and Anna. The pair had chosen Albinus and Anna's brother Viktor as witnesses. The ceremony was over in an hour and the party then dispersed to get on with their daily duties. Like the others, Ulrich and Anna changed into everyday clothes and went to work. Anna busied herself with the flat in the Church Square that Ulrich had rented for 360 francs a year. They had purchased furniture in Brig a few weeks earlier and had had it brought up by train.

Ulrich immediately went back to work building further avalanche barriers for the railway. Farming ended for him that year. His father, by now 67 and many times a grandfather, had sold his cows and sheep and gone into well-deserved retirement. His four oldest children were married, and Berta and Monika were planning to wed the following year. Franziska was employed away from Zermatt and Medard worked as a porter in the mountains while preparing for the guides' exam. The youngest daughter, Veronika, ran her father's house.

Now that he no longer had to bring in the harvest Ulrich could start work as a guide at the beginning of the season. Most of his clients had engaged him the previous year, among them Mr and Mrs May from Berlin. Slowly Ulrich was accumulating regular customers. Nevertheless, the 1930s were a difficult time for him and his colleagues.

Since 1932 the number of overnight visitors had been dropping, and markedly fewer foreigners were coming to Zermatt. The proportion of visitors from Britain dropped from more than 30% in the 1920s to below 10% in the 1930s. The guides were forced to look for other ways of earning money in autumn, winter and spring, but this was becoming steadily more difficult. Work on the railway had been completed so it

Ulrich's marriage certificate

was no longer a source of income. Leaving Zermatt to seek work was also unthinkable because the number of unemployed in the valley and other places was far too high.

So Ulrich made a virtue of necessity. He fell back on his savings and used the time of unemployment to build his own house. Anna and her brother Viktor owned a piece of land behind the village hall on the right-hand side of the Triftbach, one of the streams that run through Zermatt. There, in September 1933, Ulrich began work with his brother-in-law

Unser Hochzeitsfoto   Our marriage picture

on a two-family house. First they spent several weeks excavating the foundations. Then they looked for sand and stones for the walls. They found stones on the banks of the Vispa below the village. These were roughly shaped on the spot and deposited in a pile. Sand the two men shovelled from the river where it enters the village at Zen Stecken. Then they piled it up and left it until winter.

From December to February Viktor had to resume work as an engine driver on the Gornergrat Railway. During this period Viktor's brother Peter-Josef helped Ulrich with the building work. In January Ulrich rented a mule in Törbel, a small village above Stalden, in order to transport the sand and stones by sledge to the site. He rode the train to Stalden and there took possession of the stubborn beast, which he drove with some difficulty 17 miles back to Zermatt. In the following weeks the mule was hitched to the sledge every day and the sand and stones were loaded and dragged to the building site. When the work was completed Ulrich took the mule back to Stalden and paid the owner the agreed rental.

Mules from Törbel played an important part in the life of the valley: "The mule drivers of Törbel are much valued everywhere. Before the railway to Zermatt was built they arranged most of the transport to the valley and earned very good money. Today a muleteer can earn 400–500 francs in 2–3 months in the summer if he is thrifty. Admittedly, taking mules up the mountains, for instance to the Matterhorn hut, is heavy work, not only for the animal but also for the owner who, after the day's work and again next morning, must feed and clean the mules."[26]

As soon as the spring sun had melted the snow in the village Ulrich and his brother-in-law could start building the foundations and cellar, helped by a qualified mason.

On 4 April 1934 Anna gave birth to their first child, a girl, who was christened Maria, after Ulrich's mother. The birth took place at home with the assistance of a midwife.

That summer Ulrich's services as guide were in little demand, so he spent much time collecting material for his new house. Wood for the roof timbers could be bought at a good price from the local authority, whose forester told them which larches they could fell. The logs were at first stored in the wood below Stafelalp to be brought down after the first snowfall. Since each family was entitled to only six or seven trees they

Our daughter Maria

had to buy additional wood from the sawmill in Naters. This was then transported to Zermatt on the railway.

Slates for the roof were cut by the two men from suitable layers of rock above Zmutt. They weighed several tonnes and were initially left where they had been cut. Stone slabs for the steps were gathered from a small lake below the Gornergrat. Together the two men slid the heavy blocks to the railway and loaded them onto the train.

In the winter months the timber and stones were brought to the building site by sledge. For these heavy loads the postman made available

Auf Arbeitssuche

Looking for work

his two mules, which were no longer needed to deliver post because the railway from the valley had started an all-season service the previous October.

In the spring of 1935 it was finally time to bring in the carpenter to help with the woodwork and the roof. In June the house was ready for occupation. Ulrich and Anna moved into the apartment on the first floor while Viktor and his wife occupied the second floor. The total cost of the house was about 12,000 francs, including materials and wages for the mason, plumber, heating engineer and joiner.

With that, Ulrich's savings were exhausted. Summer again brought little work, and his financial situation deteriorated. The only customers were his friends from Berlin, who engaged him for a few expeditions.

Anna had her second child on 14 August, a son named German-Ulrich, so a family of four now had to be fed. In the off-season Ulrich therefore took any work he could find. He helped with the construction of ski runs and avalanche barriers. He worked in the forests and for the local authority. Throughout the 1930s he found no employment as a ski guide except for the one tour on which he had broken his leg. In the summer months he and his family moved into a little room under the roof and let their apartment to tourists.

A photo from this time shows Ulrich exactly as Emil Yung had described the Zermatt guides in 1893: "The guides are recognizable by their grey woollen suits, their emaciated bodies, their clear, open faces, and their generally modest, gentle expressions. They hold their heads very upright, for they are accustomed to looking much up to the sky."

In 1936 the Swiss franc was devalued. The favourable impact on the tourist industry can be seen from the many entries in Ulrich's book, including five ascents of the Matterhorn, of which two were made without the usual overnight stay in the Hörnli hut. On these occasions Ulrich started out from Zermatt with his client at about ten o'clock at night and reached the summit in the early morning, returning to the village in the afternoon.

The year brought sad news to the family from St Niklausen. Martha had died at the age of only 34. Ulrich thus lost the sister who had been closest to him. It was Martha for whom he had been responsible as a child and with whom he had made that unforgettable first ascent of the Matterhorn.

In the autumn Ulrich was called up for his last military refresher course. Since he had little desire to leave his wife and children he went to his doctor and faked stomach pains in the hope of being spared this burdensome duty. But the doctor's certificate was not regarded as

With Maria and Ulrich-German on the balcony of our house

sufficient, so Ulrich had to be examined by the military doctor in St Niklaus. This man, observing a patient who appeared to be doubled up with pain, diagnosed acute appendicitis. For Ulrich there was now no way back. On doctor's orders he went immediately to the hospital in Brig and had his healthy appendix removed, exchanging the two-week military training course for 10 days in hospital and a superfluous operation.

A few month later, at the age of 37, Ulrich rode for the first time in a car. With Medard he was asked to search for a climber who had disappeared after descending from the Dom in the direction of Saas Fee. The brothers took the train to St Niklaus, where they were met by a colleague who was the proud possessor of a motor car. The road from Stalden to St Niklaus had just been finished in 1937, though another 35 years were to pass before it was extended to Täsch, 4 miles from Zermatt.

The narrow, twisting road to Saas Fee turned the happily awaited car trip into a disappointment. Ulrich and Medard became so sick that the car had to keep stopping for them, and they arrived late at their destination. The search for the missing climber failed. Not until 16 years later did the glacier release his body.

"In the Second World War I spent 1,000 days in military service."

The number of foreign tourists in Zermatt rose encouragingly in 1937 and 1938. Ulrich led climbers from England, the United States, France and new Zealand.

In the summer of 1939, twenty-five years after the start of the First World War, history repeated itself. News of the imminent outbreak of hostilities caused foreign tourists to leave early. The guides accompanied their regular clients to the station to say goodbye, in many cases for the last time.

On 3 September general mobilization was declared in the Church Square in Zermatt and all men eligible for service were conscripted. In the four months to the end of the year Ulrich spent 51 days on active service. Like his father before him, he became a sergeant of the guard in Zermatt.

Before the end of the year a death notice arrived from Germany. Ulrich's long-time regular client from Berlin, Richard May, who had remained faithful throughout the difficult 1930s, had been killed in action.

A few months after the outbreak of war food was rationed. On government orders Zermatt had to cultivate every available piece of land in order to make the 1,144 inhabitants less dependent on imports. But the economic situation of the villagers was much better than in the First World War. Swiss tourists compensated for the absent foreigners, and the number of guests rose slightly, even during those war years.

Course for summer climbing 6–28 September 1940.
Mr Ulrich Inderbinen served as technical assistant. His outstanding technical competence, inexhaustible strength and quiet manner make him an excellent mountain guide. He is very well suited to being an instructor...

However, because of the discounts that had been introduced, the hotels and railways made modest losses. The guides suffered more heavily because their regular clients had been mostly from England and were now absent for several years.

In order to earn a living Ulrich and many of his colleagues volunteered for active service. The pay was 7–8 francs a day; those who brought their own skis and rucksacks received an additional two francs for wear and tear on their personal property.

In 1940 Ulrich spent more than 100 days on active service, mostly as a sergeant of the guard in Zermatt. In addition he gave an avalanche course, worked as technical assistant on a course for summer mountaineering and as an instructor on a high alpine course.

In the third year of the war Ulrich was at the army's disposal for 170 days and again took part in various courses. For a few weeks he was sent

High Mountain Patrol Course 15.4–21.5.41. The guide Ulrich Inderbinen served between the above dates as a technical instructor. He showed himself to be an excellent teacher, patient and indefatigable. Because of the bad weather that accompanied the whole course and brought much snow it was frequently necessary to break new trails. Inderbinen always undertook this work voluntarily and carefully. Inderbinen is an excellent mountain and ski guide. He is also modest, willing to serve and drily humorous.

1941 On active service on the Simplon

to guard the frontier passes above Saas Fee and Simplon. Little time remained for his family.

In the summer of 1942 Ulrich undertook several climbs with Swiss clients after completing five weeks of active service and two winter mountain courses of several weeks each.

The following year he spent with customs officials on the frontier at the Testa Grigia pass above Zermatt. Ulrich worked in shifts of four hours in the day and four hours at night. On his night shifts he patrolled alone from the Theodul Glacier via Schwarzsee and Stafelalp down to Zmutt. To defend himself he carried a rifle and bayonet. He was not allowed to use his torch even in the pitch dark. The village, too, was blacked out. In the evenings all windows had to be covered with black cloth.

In this period Ulrich was hired as a guide by Werner Kunz, one of the regular clients he had had for many years. They climbed the Matterhorn with Medard, who had started his own family two years earlier. Veronika had also been married for the past year. Only Franziska still lived with their father as his housekeeper.

In 1944 Ulrich spent 187 days on active service. In the final year of the war he served four months continuously until the end of the year. By the end of the war he had served altogether about 1,000 days, including all his various courses. His modest but regular army wages enabled him to support his wife and children.

Today, step by step, the "mountain of mountains" sank under us without, however, becoming any smaller. We shall not forget the brothers Ulrich and Medard Inderbinen, who were excellent guides, and whom we shall always recommend whenever the occasion arises.

After the end of the war life in Zermatt improved steadily. As early as 1945 the BVZ carried 265,000 passengers. Better times also arrived at last for the guides. They were in demand not only in summer but as ski guides and instructors from December to spring. In 1960 there were more overnight visitors in winter than in summer. The days were gone when winter meant that the men of the village had to look desperately for work elsewhere.

In the off-season new jobs were created by the construction of hotels, guest houses, apartments, ski runs, ski lifts and cable cars. Ulrich could now find work without difficulty in autumn and spring, whether as a forester on the ski runs, as mason, joiner or electrician. Thanks to his regular clients he was also well occupied in summer. In winter he worked as a ski guide, and when the weather was good he took clients almost every day on the much-loved ski tour over the Italian border to Cervinia. In spring he accompanied groups of up to six people on the Haute Route from Saas Fee to Chamonix, which took a week.

Thus, after the Second World War, Ulrich and his family enjoyed a life without worry for the first time. Yet his memories of these good years are not as vivid as those of his difficult childhood and youth. Nor has he forgotten the regular clients with whom he shares so many memories. He took some of them more than 50 times up "four-thousanders". Only once was one of his clients hurt. On the Matterhorn a man broke his arm as he was struck by a falling stone.

In all those years Ulrich himself had only one accident as guide in summer. In August 1958 his client slipped on a snowfield and fell while descending the Italian ridge of the Matterhorn. Ulrich held the man on the rope and stopped the fall but the violent jerk dislocated his shoulder. Two colleagues who had seen the accident wrenched the joint back into place and bound his arm. Medical treatment was unnecessary but for the first and last time in his 70-year career as a mountain guide he had to take a few days off.

For the last 50 years of his work Ulrich no longer needed references in his Guide's Book. The entries are therefore incomplete, making it im-

Auf dem Gipfel des Matterhorn

On the summit of the Matterhorn

Als Waldarbeiter beim Pistenbau

As a forester clearing ski trails

possible to calculate exactly how many times he has climbed the Matterhorn. He himself estimates that he has stood at least 370 times on the summit of "the most beautiful mountain in the world". Only once did he see the tracks of chamois in new snow on the summit.

Until his eightieth year he worked in the off-season for eight hours a day in a joinery. At 82 he started competing in ski races and was always the first (and only) competitor in his age group. At 84 he took a client up the Mont Blanc, at 87 up the Dufourspitze, the highest peak of the Swiss alps.

At the age of 90 he climbed the Matterhorn for the last time during the celebrations of the 125th anniversary of the first ascent. According to an account in the *Alpine Journal,* he reached the summit only four hours after leaving the Hörnli Hut. "Not surprisingly, he was the centre of many admirers and much media attention that evening during a reception outside the Zermatterhof Hotel."[27]

In spite of all the publicity and the many records he has broken, Ulrich remains modest and unassuming. Except for short trips to Frankfurt and Berlin he has never had a holiday. Nor has he ever seen the sea, nor owned a car, bicycle or telephone. "I am the only person in Zermatt without a telephone," he says.

Anyone wanting to meet Ulrich knows that he cannot be reached by telephone but is to be found every afternoon between five and six o'clock in Zermatt's Church Square. Everybody also knows that he never forgets an appointment, is always punctual, and usually arrives five minutes before the agreed time.

Many of the habits he acquired in childhood have remained with him into old age. Before he leaves the house and before he goes to bed he crosses himself with holy water. He rises early and goes to Mass every day at 8 a.m. He carries his rosary with him all the time. For decades Ulrich has had his regular place in church and never misses High Mass on Sundays. When he cuts bread he first scratches a cross on the underside of the loaf, as his mother did. He never throws old bread away – the harder it is the better he likes it. His apartment is heated with wood that he splits himself. He regards the logs as valuable objects that should be used sparingly.

Ulrich has not lost the dry humour that is often mentioned in his Guide's Book. He laughs easily and enjoys perplexing others in conversation.

When strangers mention the many newspaper articles written about him he insists firmly that he is not the famous mountain guide but his twin brother. If one asks him if he regrets anything in his life he tells with mock resignation of a journey he could not undertake – a climb up Kilimanjaro at the age of 92 that was strongly opposed by his family. "I really have no idea why they were all against it," he sighs.

Even today Ulrich is still amused by the reaction of some guests who were sent to him a few years ago by the Zermatter Mountain Guides Office without being told of his age. One of them complained, saying he feared he might have to carry the 87-year-old guide up the Dufourspitze. After the climb the guest revised his opinion and asked in future for a guide who would occasionally allow him a break.

One day at the age of 91 Ulrich was seen carrying two pairs of skis to the Klein Matterhorn cable car. A tourist asked him why he needed two pairs. "The second pair belongs to my father who's just behind," replied Ulrich, deadpan.

A Swiss television interviewer once asked him on a live show: "Did you really come all by yourself on the train to Zurich?". Ulrich replied: "No, there were a few other people on the train."

Another journalist asked Ulrich whether he was afraid of death. "Not really," replied the old man. "When I look at the death notices in the paper I scarcely ever see anyone of my age."

Epilogue

Over the past few months we have learnt a lot about – and from – Ulrich Inderbinen. We feel personally enriched by our talks and walks and all the time we spent with him.

Ulrich's history exemplifies that of Zermatt in the first half of this century. Like him and his family, the rest of the local people lived a life of privation until, towards the end of the 1940s, economic growth started.

In Ulrich's home village there are now 114 hotels and 1,500 holiday apartments which in 1995 counted more than 1.5 million overnight stays. Altogether about 1.4 million people visit Zermatt every year, making it Switzerland's favourite mountain resort. In the high season as many as 8,000 tourists arrive each day.

The village has about 5,500 inhabitants, of whom a third are foreigners, as are most of the 1,800 seasonal workers employed by hotels, restaurants and shops in the summer and winter seasons.

Zermatt allows no cars, so electric taxis and buses take visitors to the hotels, apartments and bottom stations of the mountain railways and cable cars. The transport system now includes the venerable but modernised Gornergrat Railway, an underground funicular and numerous cable cars and chairlifts which take people comfortably to the skiing and walking areas.

At present there are 60 mountain guides and 175 ski instructors whose services can be booked at the Mountain Guide Office and the Ski School. Mountain rescues are assisted by helicopters so the injured can be transported in a few minutes to one of Zermatt's five doctors or to the hospitals in Visp and Brig.

In spite of the breakneck speed of development and the many innovations, Zermatt has been able to conserve some of its original character. In some places time seems to have stood still. The old barns, storehouses and cowsheds have been restored, and the mountain hamlets have remained relatively untouched. In Blatten, Zmutt and Herbrigg one can still get a feeling for Ulrich's past life. On the mountain slopes above the village the fields where rye once grew are still visible.

Down below, the old Zermatt is still to be found, mainly in the back streets. Clean drinking water flows from the fountain where Ulrich's mother did her laundry, just as it did 100 years ago. Even the cowshed belonging to the Inderbinen family stands unchanged opposite the fountain.

The Haus Vispa, built in 1900, has been renovated. The Haus Am Bach that Ulrich built, and in which he has lived for 61 years, is still in excellent condition. Only the roof had to be replaced a while ago.

On 12 December 1984 Ulrich's wife Anna died after 51 years of marriage. Since then his daughter Maria has run the house. His son German-Ulrich lives next door with his wife. Ulrich is twice a great-grandfather.

In his home village he has become a symbolic and respected figure. The village is proud of this apparently indestructible old man who embodies like no other the traditional profession of mountain guide and the values associated with it. Ulrich is disciplined and absolutely reliable. He has respect for the mountains, knows no false ambition and never takes risks.

In spite of his age he is a living contradiction of everything that one associates with the world "old". Whereas age is often equated with declining physical and mental ability, Ulrich is open, active and enjoys a phenomenal memory. His charisma inspires journalists to write of his "purity of soul". He has dignity and wisdom – words that have nowadays almost disappeared from daily use.

Many changes have passed him by without altering his character or his simple way of life. On the whole he welcomes the development of his home village but he has little sympathy with the side-effects of prosperity:

"In the old days life was hard but good. Everyone had little and helped everyone else. People were more content than they are today. Nowadays they have everything and think only of themselves."

Ulrich with Pope John Paul II, 24 April 1996

The British in Zermatt (by Richard Davy)

The British have had a special relationship with Zermatt since long before Edward Whymper conquered the Matterhorn in 1865. The first recorded British visitor was George Cade from York, who arrived in 1800 with a guide, causing a sensation among the villagers. The local priest said he had never seen an Englishman before.

Within a few decades the British had become familiar in Zermatt. Easier travel and the spread of railways, which reached Switzerland in 1844, had made the Alps increasingly fashionable among the Aristocracy and professional classes.

Although the British gathered in many other Alpine resorts, none fascinated them as deeply as Zermatt. Whymper's exploit,[28] generated a lot of publicity and the fact that four of his party died on the Matterhorn – the first of several hundred deaths on the mountain – seemed if anything to increase the attraction of Zermatt. The village became, in words of Francois Gos, a "spiritual home" of the Alpine Club, founded in 1857. Arnold Lunn has described the awe with which he watched the members of the Alpine Club taking their places at the table traditionally reserved for the Club. "For civilized mountaineers", he wrote, "the Monte Rosa is also a shrine, dedicated to the memory of the early Fathers of the Mountain Faith".[29]

The *Times* carried a lengthy correspondence on every aspect of Whymper's expedition but was not easily converted to mountaineering, asking sceptically "But is it life? Is it duty? Is it common sense?"[30] Nevertheless, it continued to carry regular reports from the village, mentioning, for instance, an earthquake in 1880, improvements to the drainage system in 1901, the first winter season in 1929, a highway robbery and fairly regular accidents to climbers.

British writers were inspired to heights of lyricism by the Matterhorn. John Ruskin described it rather confusingly as "standing like an Egyptian temple – delicate-fronted, softly coloured, the suns of uncounted ages rising and falling upon it continually, but still casting the same line of shadows from east to west..."[31]

Perhaps the most prolific mountaineer writer was W.A.B. Coolidge, a somewhat eccentric Oxford don who was a frequent visitor to Zermatt. Known as "the Boswell of the Alps" he wrote countless books, guides and articles. He also became famous for taking his dog Tschingel on 66 major climbs and about 100 minor ones.

Many British travellers brought their families with them. The women in long skirts, the men often in suits and ties, reached peaks and glaciers with equipment that today's climbers would regard as dangerously inadequate. Some women became expert climbers in their own right. The first woman to climb the Matterhorn was Lucy Walker, who made the ascent in 1871, just before Mr Coolidge's aunt and frequent climbing companion Meta Brevoort, who is also reported to have danced a quadrille with her guide on the summit of Mont Blanc.[32]

Most British visitors came for the challenge of mountaineering or the pleasures of mountain walking, but it was also a time of expanding intellectual curiosity, when Darwin's new theories of evolution were shifting the foundations of science and religion. Earnest schoolteachers, clergymen, doctors and scientists would arrive in Zermatt with bulky surveying equipment, primitive cameras and, above all, notebooks in which they recorded their meticulous observations and lofty sentiments. Some looked for the secrets of nature in the slow evolution of the plants, rocks and glaciers, others for the hand of God in the majesty of the peaks. The first editor of the *Alpine Journal* from 1863, the Reverend Hereford Brooke George, wrote that climbing was the means by which men could see more clearly "that above and beyond all laws rises the supreme will of the Almighty lawgiver".[33]

By the second half of the nineteenth century so many British visitors were coming to Zermatt that they needed their own church. "The Victorian gentleman travelling in Europe," wrote Cicely Williams in *A Church in the Alps,* "liked to have his accustomed comforts around him, more especially when the family was present. Among the requirements he deemed necessary was divine worship in the form of full matins and evensong – the later shortened if the mountains were in good condition!... Parsons were numerous among mountaineers at that time – in fact some of the best climbers of the day came from the ranks of the clergy – and it was comparatively easy to find someone to conduct Sunday services. A more difficult problem was to provide sufficient accommodation for those who wished to attend. In 1858 regular services were held in the lounges of the Monte Rosa and the Hotel des Alpes, but as numbers increased conditions became more and more congested".

An approach was therefore made to the Colonial and Continental Church Society. Fund-raising started early in 1865, and five years later the church was open. It remains in operation today.

Winter holidays did not become popular until the railway started a winter service in 1929, but, many years before that, hardy British skiers would walk up the valley. In 1908 Arnold Lunn inspired a group of Englishmen to found the Alpine Ski Club, although ski mountaineering was still regarded by many as "the folly of irresponsible youth and was summarily dismissed" according to the British mountaineer C. Scott Lindsay. "At that time," he wrote, "it was no light achievement to get up the valley from Visp to Zermatt loaded with an immense rucksack and the long ski then in use, 2.5m. That occupied the whole of a long, hard day, and on arrival the shock was total. Up to then Zermatt had not been visited in winter by persons interested in the mountains and armed with skis. The entire community was spending the long winter months in peaceful hibernation, and there was absolutely no provision for visitors. We managed to find beds in a chalet and then lived for some four weeks almost solely on goat's meat, goat's cheese, and goat's milk, accompanied by bread baked in the autumn to last the winter. Since then I have never been able to look a goat in the face, much less to eat one, but that was the true Zermatt. We did little more than reconnoitre the glaciers and we made the first ski ascent of the Adler Pass. In doubtful weather we made an attempt to show the younger guides something of skiing; little did they then think that they could not live today but for their earnings as *ski-lehrer*."[34]

Since then the British presence in Zermatt has fluctuated in response to wars, currency restrictions and rates of exchange, but it has seldom been less than significant in peacetime. In recent years the British have made up about 6 % of summer visitors and 8 % of winter visitors with a substantial influx for the crazy but enjoyable Luttman-Johnson race, run annually by the Ski Club of Great Britain. This requires contestants to check in at a number of the delightful mountain restaurants that dot the slopes above Zermatt. Very sensibly, in order to appreciate one of the best features of the resort, they have to spend as much time as possible in each restaurant before racing hectically to the next.

From time to time, too, one can encounter British visitors sporting a badge awarded to them by the Zermatt authorities for having visited the resort every year for 20 years. They are the most faithful representatives of a long tradition.

Footnotes

1 Re-printed in Theodor Wundt, *Das Matterhorn und seine Geschichte,* Kgl. Hofbuchdruckerei, Stuttgart o.J., p.31.

2 In the summer season the larger hotels hired a doctor exclusively for the benefit of tourists.

3 F.A.Volmar, *Gornergrat-Chronik,* Verlag Orell Füssli AG, Zürich 1958, p.29.

4 A reference to Thebes, the magnificent ancient city on the Upper Nile.

5 Seiler Hotels, *Zermatt. Dorf und Kurort im Spiegel einer Familie.* Visp 1982, p.79.

6 *Journal de Zermatt,* October 1906. (The Journal de Zermatt was founded in 1891)

7 Gaston Rébuffat, *Matterhorn. Belle Epoque,* Grands Vents 1983, p.69. See also Paul Lehner, *75 Jahre Skiclub Zermatt 1908–1983,* p.13, and *Festschrift zum 100-Jahr-Jubiläum der Sektion Monte Rosa des SAC,* p.141.

8 Theodor Wundt, op. cit., p.115.

9 In literature, Blatten is often described as an abandoned village, and even in 1900 it was empty during three-quarters of the year. Stanislaus Kronig, *Familien-Statistik und Geschichtliches über die Gemeinde Zermatt,* Päpstl. Theodosius-Buchdruckerei, 1927, p.206; Francois Gos, *Zermatt und sein Tal,* Verlag Alpina, Genf, 1925, p.108 and Albert Gos, *Souvenirs d'un peintre de montagne,* J.-H. Jeheber S.A., Geneve 1942, p.83.

10 Georg Julen, *Wörterbuch der Zermatter Mundart,* Rotten-Verlag, Brig 1985.

11 Albert Gos, op. cit., p. 85f.

12 In earlier times there had been a surplus of wood. Stanislaus Kronig, op. cit., p.233. See also *Journal de Zermatt,* 1907, nr.12, *Das veränderte Klima im Wallis:* "In Zermatt the powerful glacier which can now be seen from Zermatt, once looked as small as a white goat, and where now the massive glaciers pile up, there were formerly such thickets, that mules got lost in them."

13 Quotations from the Bible are taken from the Douay-Rheims translation of 1582–1610 which was used by English-speaking Catholics in the period of Ulrich's schooldays. It does not always correspond precisely with the German translation used in this catechism.

14 Arnold Lunn, *The Alps,* Thornton Butterworth, 1914, p.148.

15 Skiing was, however, starting to arrive. In March 1898, Oscar Schuster, a German, made the first ski ascent of Monte Rosa. In 1902 Dr Hermann Seiler, son of Alexander Seiler, organised ski courses for Zermatt guides. According to Francois Gos, 14 July 1911 was an "epoch making day in the history of Zermatt" because it marked the first successful ski run from Bourg-St-Pierre to Zermatt, a tour later extended to become the famous and much-travelled Haute Route from Chamonix to Zermatt. (F. Gos, op.cit.)

16 Samuel Brawand, *Mein altes Zermatt,* Manuscript, p.2.

17 F.G. Stebler, *Monographien über das Oberwallis um 1900,* Facsimile, Verlag Neue Buchdruckerei Visp, 1981, p.109.

18 At Riffelalp a second Anglican church, the "Holy Trinity Church", was inaugurated on 27 July 1884.

19 Edward A. Broome, *Zermatt in War-Time,* in: *Alpine Journal,* May 1916, p.139. Edward Broome (1845–1920) is buried in the English churchyard of Zermatt. For the epitaph on his gravestone a couplet from Romeo and Juliet was chosen: "Night's candles are burnt out And jocund day stands tiptoe on the misty mountain tops".

20 F. Schwarz, *Erinnerungen an Zermatt,* in: *Alpina,* 1916.

21 F. Gos, op.cit.

22 Dr Montagu Butler was described by *The Times* as "a brilliant scholar and eminent divine", he was a remarkable man, a great classicist, liberal thinker and friend of many famous people, including Tennyson, Matthew Arnold, John Ruskin and Charles Kingsley. (see Leading article in *The Times,* 2 November 1886)

23 A.L.M., *Alpine Journal,* November 1926, nr. 233, 300–302.

24 Sir Arnold Lunn, *A Century of Mountaineering 1857–1957,* Allen and Unwin, London 1965 and *Zermatt and the Valais,* Hollis and Carter, London 1955.

25 *Alpine Journal,* May 1957.

26 F.G. Stebler, op. cit., p.56.

27 John Hunt, *Alpine Journal* 1991/92, p.132-4. (Lord Hunt was leader of the expedition that enabled Edmund Hillary and Sherpa Tensing to make the first ascent of Mount Everest in 1953.)

28 His own account appears in *Scrambles amongst the Alps in the years 1860–1869,* Murray, 1871.

29 Sir Arnold Lunn, *A History of Skiing,* Oxford University Press, 1927.

30 Quoted in Ronald Clark, op. cit.

31 John Ruskin, *Modern Painters,* vol. IV. Quoted in *The Englishman in the Alps,* edited by Arnold Lunn, Oxford University Press, 1913.

32 Women continued to climb from Zermatt. For a lively account of climbing in the 1920s see Janet Adam Smith, *Mountain Holidays,* The Ernest Press, 1996.

33 Ronald Clark, *The Victorian Mountaineers,* B.T. Batsford, 1953.

34 The British Ski Year-book, vol. XVII 1956-7.

Sources

Many of the pictures reproduced in this book belong to Ulrich Inderbinen's private collection. In addition we would like to thank the following persons and institutions:

for photographs
In Zermatt: German Inderbinen and Ivo Kronig, Ariette Biner-Inderbinen, Helmut Biner (Kurverein Zermatt), Willy Hofstetter (Museum Zermatt), Medard Inderbinen, Stefanie Inderbinen, Barbara and Bruno Perren-Barberini.

In addition: Alpine Club Library, London, (Mr. Peter Ledeboer); Eidgenössisches Archiv für Denkmalpflege, Bern – Collections Wehrli und Zinggeler (Frau Born/Herr Moser); Kantonsbibliothek Sitten; Musée de L'Elysée Lausanne (Herr Blaser); Photo Klopfenstein, Adelboden; Schweizerische Landesbibliothek Bern – Sektion Grafische Sammlungen (Frau Parris); Staatsarchiv Sitten – Collection Emil Gos; Walliser Film- und Fotoarchiv, Martinach; Zentralbibliothek Zürich – Sektion Graphische Sammlungen (Frau Rutz), Bernhard Clemenz, Stalden, and Marianne Wespi, Grächen.

for dokuments:
René Biner, Zivilstandsamt Zermatt; Bernhard Truffer, Staatsarchiv Sitten; Pfarrarchiv Zermatt.

Warm thanks also to Stefan Brantschen for the "Canisi", Willy Hofstetter, Maria Inderbinen, German Inderbinen, Medard Inderbinen and Ivo Kronig for oral information, Stefanie Inderbinen, Owen Hickey and Adam Roberts for advice on translation, Moritz Inderbinen, Menziken, who made available his grandfather's Guide's Book, Paul Lehner for the "School Booklet" and the manuscript of the Radio Matterhorn broadcast, Oswald Perren and the Zermatt Kurverein for more recent newspaper articles, Erich Weilenmann for the copy of the postcard on page 51, the friendly and always helpful staff of the Canton Library in Sitten, the artist Silvano Armanini, who designed the back cover for the book and to the libraries of the Ski Club of Great Britain and the School of Geography, Oxford University.